EASY
VEGAN
BIBLE

200 Easiest Ever Plant-Based Recipes

KATY BESKOW

Photography by Luke Albert

Hardie Grant

QUADRILLE

Introduction

When I became vegan back in 2006, the recipes I found seemed lacklustre. Ingredients were often difficult to source as well as being confusing and time-consuming to prepare. So, I set out on a mission to create the most vibrant and delicious home-cooked food I could whip up, on a budget, with time constraints, and with very minimal kitchen equipment. This way of cooking allowed me to create hearty, balanced, flavourful food, with a fast cooking time (and less washing up!), without breaking the bank, and with very little effort.

Fast-forward to the present, and British supermarket shelves are stocked with vegan-friendly ingredients, ready meals, condiments and clearly labelled products to suit every budget. While it is wonderful that the vegan lifestyle is now truly within the mainstream market and media, and accessible to so many people, it is important to get in the kitchen and cook meals with fresh ingredients, rather than solely relying on vegan convenience food. This way you can create balanced, home-cooked meals, create less waste from food packaging, and feel confident to experiment with new ingredients. A good way of cooking is to utilize some pre-prepared ingredients along with fresh ingredients, and to use what's available seasonally.

I know from personal experience that it's not always easy to get in the kitchen to cook something from scratch, as real life can get in the way, so I've put together this book of 200 recipes that are quick, easy and effortless, for those times when you can't commit to hours in the kitchen. Let these easy recipes help you fall in love with plant-based cooking, especially when you have limited time (and inclination) to prepare a meal from scratch.

Easy Vegan Bible shows you how to cook simple, fast and delicious food with minimal effort, using ingredients available from your local supermarket. It's also pretty likely that you'll already have many of the ingredients in your store cupboard. I've also included easy tips throughout to help you get the most out of your time in the kitchen. Many of the recipes are suitable for freezing, so you can batch cook or conveniently freeze a portion for another time. There are six chapters in the book: Breakfast & Brunch, Lunch, Supper, Something Special, Sweet, and Sides & Useful Bits. And within each chapter you'll find recipes that are ready in 15 minutes, ready in 30 minutes, use just one pot, or can be made with five ingredients.

I'm so delighted to bring you this collection of tried and tested recipes that I love to cook at home. I hope it introduces you to new ingredients and shows you how to get the best from familiar fresh ingredients and trusted store cupboard essentials. Most importantly, I hope the recipes become part of your regular repertoire, even if you are not a confident or adventurous home cook.

Whether you are a new or established vegan, vegetarian, flexitarian, or just looking for fresh ways to cook, let *Easy Vegan Bible* be your guide to creating simple, feel-good food for every craving and occasion.

How to use *Easy Vegan Bible*

There are six chapters of recipes within this book, taking you from breakfast to supper, whether you fancy a simple lunch, or are planning a special dinner.

Breakfast & Brunch – Sweet and savoury recipes to start your day in a balanced way.

Lunch – From packed lunch essentials to relaxed weekend lunches.

Supper – Cosy, comfort food that is easy to whip up for weeknight meals.

Something Special – Celebrate those special times with a wonderful dinner.

Sweet – Desserts, bakes, classics and twists on your favourite puddings.

Sides & Useful Bits – Perfect side dishes, condiments and useful recipes to have in your repertoire.

Within each chapter, the recipes are split into four categories so you can decide what to cook based on the time and ingredients you have available – and how much washing up you want to do!

15 MINUTE · MINUTE · MINUTE

These recipes have minimal preparation, and a cooking time of 15 minutes or less, without compromising on delicious flavour.

30 MINUTE · MINUTE · MINUTE

The perfect recipes for when you have only half an hour to spare in the kitchen, but want to create something easy and satisfying.

1 POT · POT · POT · POT

Whether it's cooked in a pot or a roasting tray, these recipes use just one cooking dish (and minimal utensils), meaning less for you to wash up!

5 INGREDIENTS · INGREDIENTS

Each of these recipes uses just five ingredients (occasionally fewer). Oil, salt and pepper aren't included within the count as you'll already have these in your store cupboard.

Essential kitchen equipment

You don't need to own the latest new kitchen gadget to cook great food. A few simple pieces of equipment make preparation and cooking quick and effortless, and in some cases can reduce food waste.

POTS, PANS AND TRAYS

As a rule, a couple of medium and large pans, alongside a wok, frying (skillet) and griddle (grill) pan will help you to cook versatile meals. A heavy-based, hob-to-table casserole dish is an excellent investment, particularly if you enjoy one-pot cooking. A deep roasting tray will allow you to cook a meal in the oven while you do other things – like the roasted fajitas on page 159. To make your pots and pans last longer, clean with washing-up liquid and warm water and avoid the use of scratchy cleansing pads, which can damage non-stick linings.

KNIVES

Your home kitchen does not need a big selection of knives: one small, medium and large, as well as a bread knife, will serve your needs. Buy the best you can afford for an investment that will last well into the future. Choose knives that are comfortable and ergonomic for you and look after them by using wooden chopping boards.

FREEZER-FRIENDLY CONTAINERS

Reduce food waste by freezing leftovers in containers, or batch cook when you have the time (you'll thank your past self later!) Allow your food to cool fully in individual containers, then securely cover with the lid. Be sure to label and date the container with what is inside, as the contents won't be easy to recognize when frozen. As a general rule, home-cooked meals will freeze for up to 3 months before losing quality. You can buy containers cheaply from home essentials shops, and reuse them multiple times. Cook up a pot of Italian barley stew with white beans and greens (page 130) and freeze into portions for a quick supper served with warm, crusty bread.

MICROWAVE OVEN

Microwaves are for so much more than heating convenience food! Safely reheat your leftovers or batch cooked meals, and use your microwave to try cheat's spring risotto (page 208) followed by berry crumble in a mug (page 253).

BLENDER

High-powered jug blenders (over 1000W for the best versatility) are my first choice for whipping up the silkiest soups, desserts, sauces and smoothies. A simple stick blender is a space saver, but will require a little more time and effort to achieve a smooth result. A food processor is a useful tool if you find chopping difficult, and can also blitz up ingredients into a sauce or breadcrumb texture, similarly to a high-powered blender.

JARS

Sealed glass jars are a convenient and hygienic way to store sauces and homemade condiments in your fridge. They can be purchased from home essentials stores, or you can thoroughly wash empty jam jars and reuse them for a zero-waste approach.

UTENSILS

The basic wooden spoon is a kitchen hero. They are perfect to use when stirring hot dishes as the heat is not transferred through the wood, protecting your hands from high temperatures. They also protect your pans from scratches that can happen if using metal or plastic spoons. A slotted spoon is excellent for removing mixed tempura (page 298) from hot oil; a ladle for serving soup, a can opener and kitchen scissors for snipping fresh herbs are other essentials that won't take up too much space in your kitchen. A good-quality Y-shaped vegetable peeler is useful for creating carrot ribbons for banh mi with quick pickles (page 88) and for peeling the skin from tougher vegetables such as butternut squash.

Your shopping trolley

All of the ingredients used in this book are available in supermarkets, so finding the ingredients is just as easy as cooking them! Supermarket shopping and online grocery ordering is convenient as often everything is within one space, but do consider shopping at your local fruit and vegetable market, world food store, zero waste shop, through a waste-free website or app, or by searching for local community allotment produce share schemes, for variety, reduced waste and lower costs.

FRESH

Fruit and vegetables

Choose quality fresh produce, and where possible pick fruit and vegetables that are in season for the best flavour, texture and price. To reduce food waste, shop for versatile vegetables that can be used in many ways such as spinach, which can be added to a curry or used as a salad leaf, or celery, which can be added to a casserole base or stir-fried for extra crunch. Shop for onions, garlic, carrots and potatoes as these work well as a base for many dishes and meals, then choose the other vegetables and fruits based on seasonality and what looks vibrant.

Versatile fresh leafy herbs including basil, flat-leaf parsley and coriander (cilantro) lift the flavours of a dish in one easy step. Store them stem down in a glass of water

for longevity. Fresh lemons and limes also provide bursts of flavour to a sweet or savoury dish with very little effort; be sure to choose unwaxed varieties of any citrus fruits as the waxed varieties are glazed with a product derived from an animal source.

Keep fresh fruits and vegetables chilled or cool for freshness, then let them come back to room temperature before enjoying to bring out their best flavours and juices. Many vegetables and plant-based proteins cook well from frozen, including peas, spinach, leeks, butternut squash, sweetcorn and edamame beans.

Tofu

Tofu (made from the curds of soya) is a versatile ingredient, readily available in supermarkets. Not only is it full of protein, it's filling and easy to use (see my guide to tofu on page 21). Across this book I've used extra-firm tofu and silken tofu. Extra-firm tofu can be sliced or cubed into meaty pieces, while silken tofu makes an excellent chocolate mousse!

Shop-bought pastry

Many brands of shop-bought shortcrust, puff and filo pastry use vegetable oil instead of dairy butter in the production, making these items suitable for vegans. This can vary from brand to brand, so always check the label before you buy. Shop-bought pastry is also quick and fuss-free to use, and helps you to create a hearty dish or dessert without the effort of making your own.

NON-DAIRY

Milks

You'll find a wide range of plant-based milks in supermarkets, including oat, almond, blended coconut, and rice. I find the most versatile plant-based milk is unsweetened soya, which can be used in savoury and sweet cooking, in hot drinks and over cereals. It's worth trying a few and choosing your favourite. Most of the milks are available in long-life UHT (ultra-high temperature) packs or fresh from chillers.

Cheeses

There is now a large selection of vegan cheese available in supermarkets, and I'm often asked which is the best to use. If you're in need of a mozzarella alternative to melt on hot food, try a vegan mozzarella-style cheese; if you want a sandwich-filling hard cheese, try a cheddar alternative; if you want a cheesecake filler, try a vegan alternative to cream cheese. The ingredients vary from brand to brand, but many of the cheeses have a base of almond, soya or coconut.

Yogurt

There are many brands and flavours of vegan yogurt from classic fruit varieties to unsweetened Greek-style. Thick coconut varieties and plain unsweetened soya yogurt offer the most versatility as both can be used in savoury dishes, marinades, dips, and sweet baking.

Mayonnaise

Vegan mayonnaise is now readily available in supermarkets, and is a great addition to your store cupboard for spreading into sandwiches, using in sauces, and dips. Choose from various flavours, or stick with traditional and stir in your own additions.

Cream

Soya or oat-based pouring cream can be used in cooking and baking. It is often available in UHT varieties, so it will have a long shelf life.

Vegan butter

Vegan butter, margarine or spreads are widely available, with varying 'buttery' flavours. They all have different oil contents, which can make a difference within vegan baking. Palm oil-free varieties are now available, and some vegan butters can be bought in block form rather than a plastic container.

Canned beans and pulses

Choose a selection of canned beans and pulses including chickpeas (garbanzo beans), green lentils and red kidney beans, so you can add protein and bite to a dish with very little preparation, soaking or boiling times. These ingredients have a long shelf life, meaning they're a handy essential to have in the cupboard. Simply pour away the canned water and rinse thoroughly in cold water to avoid any tell-tale canned taste.

Dried pulses, grains and rice

Have a few varieties of dried pulses and grains available including dried red lentils, bulgar wheat and pearl barley to thicken soups, curries and casseroles. Basmati and jasmine rice are fast cooking and have a wonderful fragrance. Oats are a staple ingredient in any kitchen, and are economical too. All of these items have a long shelf life when stored in a cool, dark cupboard.

Jackfruit

Once exclusive to Asian supermarkets, jackfruit can now be found in most large supermarkets, either canned or vacuum-packed, giving it a long life in your store cupboard. As the name suggests, jackfruit is a fruit, but it has a neutral taste, making it easy to flavour however you wish, and a meaty texture than can mimic anything from pulled pork to flaked fish. See page 22 for my guide to jackfruit.

Herb and spice blends

Alongside a selection of fresh herbs and your favourite dried herbs and spices, have a few pre-blended mixes in your store cupboard to save you time and effort when cooking. These may include curry pastes (ensure dairy-free), rose harissa, piri piri seasoning and jerk seasoning, which are expertly blended to easily add flavour and spice to any dish.

Oil

Sunflower oil is my favourite oil to cook with, as it has a mild flavour that won't overpower the ingredients, a high smoke point making it versatile for frying and roasting, and is readily available at a low cost. Extra virgin olive oil is great for dressings, drizzles and dipping, so splash out on a good-quality bottle and use it sparingly.

Sea salt and black pepper

Good-quality sea salt flakes, when used sparingly, enhance the finished flavour of any dish – just lightly crush between your fingers when sprinkling. I'd also recommended a box of smoked sea salt flakes, for a lightly smoked flavour that adds depth to many dishes. Freshly cracked black pepper is a great way to finish a dish with pops of flavour and a little heat.

Apple cider vinegar

A bottle of this versatile vinegar can be used to quick-pickle vegetables with its acidic, fresh flavour, but can also make buttermilk when stirred into soya milk – perfect for vegan baking and velvety sponge cakes.

Stock cubes

Vegetable stock (in the form of cubes, powders or fresh) gives depth to a dish, as well as being a flavourful base in homemade soups. Do check the ingredients of vegetable stocks, as some contain cow's milk and milk derivatives.

Dried pasta and noodles

Most dried pasta available in the supermarket is vegan, as it is egg-free and usually contains just semolina flour, but always check the ingredients before you buy. Avoid fresh pastas found in supermarket chillers, as they are likely to contain eggs. Similarly to pasta, avoid 'fresh' noodles which require chilled temperatures, and choose soft, ready-to-wok noodles or dehydrated noodles which are both found on supermarket shelves, but always check the ingredients to ensure that they are egg-free.

Chopped tomatoes

Chopped tomatoes are a store cupboard essential, creating a base for many casseroles, curries and sauces. Choose good-quality canned varieties, alongside cartons of passata (sieved tomatoes), and concentrated tomato purée (paste), so you're prepared to make any dish. If you find tomato dishes too acidic, add a small pinch of sugar to balance the acidity.

Canned coconut milk

From creamy curries to panna cotta, coconut milk is a great way to add a silky texture and rich flavour to so many dishes. Choose cans of full-fat coconut milk for the best flavour and texture in your cooking.

Alcohol

Wine, beer or cider can be added to a dish to give a deep, hearty flavour; or it can be enjoyed alongside your meal. Some brands and varieties of wine, beer and cider contain animal ingredients including isinglass (from the swim bladders of fish), gelatine and eggs, making them unsuitable for vegans. Some supermarkets note on the bottle label if the alcohol is suitable for vegans, or use a trusted online source.

A guide to tofu

Tofu is a versatile ingredient, made from the curds of soya milk. It can be used in a variety of ways, to be the star of a dish, or to act in a similar way to eggs in cooking. Tofu naturally has a bland flavour; however, it absorbs flavours well, meaning it can be used in many dishes. Tofu is sold in varying levels of firmness; in this book, I use extra-firm tofu and silken tofu.

Tofu can seem complicated to prepare and cook, but with a few handy hints, the process is demystified, and you can get on with enjoying tofu in all its versatile glory!

Extra-firm tofu is often found in the chiller sections of supermarkets, vacuum-packed for freshness. You may notice that is has some water surrounding it in the packet. The trick to cooking perfect extra-firm tofu is to remove as much moisture from it as possible, by draining and pressing the block. You can buy a tofu press to do this effectively, or simply wrap the tofu in kitchen paper or a clean, dry tea towel and place on a large plate. Place another plate on top of the block and add a couple of cookbooks or a heavy pan over to weigh it down. Allow to stand for 1 hour, before slicing and using as needed. Some brands of extra-firm tofu are now sold as 'pre-pressed', making the cooking of tofu even easier.

Drain and press tofu when you want to use chunky cubes or pieces of tofu that won't fall apart during cooking (or on your fork) including banh mi with quick pickles (page 88), golden-battered tofish (page 212) and southern baked goujons (page 213).

Occasionally you may want smaller pieces of tofu that break up easily. For this purpose, drain away the excess moisture from the block but there's no need to press it. Try this method for tofu-fried rice (page 185), tomato and red onion frittatas (page 56) and Mexican scrambled tofu (page 57).

Silken tofu is sold in semi-liquid form, and is best used in desserts and sauces that require a creamy base. You'll find this on the ambient shelves in large supermarkets, and in Chinese supermarkets. There's no need to press this type of tofu, which has a soft, creamy texture, just use straight from the carton. Try it in chocolate orange mousse (page 267) for a bubbly, decadent dessert.

A guide to jackfruit

As the name suggests, jackfruit is in fact a fruit, however it doesn't have a sweet flavour. Instead it has a meaty texture and mild taste, making it the perfect meat and fish substitute in vegan cooking. Jackfruit takes on flavours from marinades and sauces quickly, meaning it can be used as a quick alternative to meat, fish and other vegan alternatives.

Jackfruit can now be found in most supermarkets and Asian grocery shops. It is available canned or vacuum-packed. The preserved varieties have a meatier texture than the fresh green fruit (which can develop a sweeter flavour), and are much more convenient to use and easier to source outside Asia.

Jackfruit will usually be preserved in brine. Thoroughly drain this away before use, and rinse with plenty of fresh water to remove any salty flavours and canned taste. While rinsing the jackfruit, break up the pieces into finer strands, and discard any tough bits. Pat away the moisture before using in a recipe.

Feeling a little inspired by the meaty appeal of jackfruit? Try hoisin no-duck pancakes (page 193), Korean barbecue jackfruit tacos (page 164), sticky pulled jackfruit sandwiches (page 91) or Thai spiced no-fish pie (page 190).

Breakfast & Brunch

Autumn breakfast bowl

SERVES 1

1 fig, sliced into quarters

handful of blackberries

handful of flaked
(slivered) almonds

handful of pecans

2 rounded tbsp rolled oats

2 tbsp plain soya yogurt

drizzle of maple syrup

Feast on the colours and flavours of autumn with this balanced breakfast bowl. If you have a little time to spare, toast the almonds and pecans in a dry pan for 3–4 minutes for an extra layer of comforting flavour.

1 Put the fig quarters, blackberries, almonds and pecans into a bowl.

2 Spoon in the oats and cover with the yogurt. Drizzle a little maple syrup over the yogurt.

EASY TIP
This breakfast bowl can be made the night before and kept refrigerated until morning.

Hazelnut and sour cherry granola

MAKES ABOUT
10 SERVINGS

---

4 tbsp sunflower oil

4 tbsp maple syrup

300g (3 cups) rolled oats

50g (⅓ cup) blanched hazelnuts, roughly chopped

50g (1¾oz) dried sour cherries

Combine the delicious flavours of maple, toasted hazelnuts and sour cherries in this simple granola. This easy recipe can be altered to suit your tastes, with extra nuts, fruits and seeds, as you see fit. A jar of this granola makes an excellent gift, or just make so you always having some at hand in your store cupboard. Serve with thick coconut yogurt.

1 Preheat the oven to 160°C/325°F/gas mark 3.

2 Mix together the oil and maple syrup in a jug.

3 Combine the oats, hazelnuts and cherries in a bowl, then pour over the oil and maple syrup mixture. Stir together until everything is coated.

4 Spread the mixture out evenly over two baking trays, then bake in the oven for 40–45 minutes, stirring the mixture every 10 minutes to encourage oaty clumps to form.

5 Allow the granola to cool fully on the baking trays before sealing in clean jars. The granola will last up to 2 months

EASY TIP
Serve this granola with ice-cold almond milk, apple juice or a generous spoonful of your favourite non-dairy yogurt.

Throw-it-in muesli

SERVES 1 GENEROUSLY

4 tbsp rolled oats

1 green apple, grated

2 tbsp roughly chopped pecans

handful of plump sultanas
(golden raisins)

1 tbsp pumpkin seeds

For the mornings when you need something balanced, fresh and filling, look no further than this simple homemade muesli. The quantities are easy to increase for extra portions, or you can combine all of the ingredients, except the grated apple, to store in a sealed container for up to 3 months (add the grated apple just before serving).

1 Add all of the ingredients to a bowl and mix until evenly distributed.

EASY TIP
Serve this muesli with ice-cold almond milk, apple juice or a generous spoonful of your favourite non-dairy yogurt.

Apple pie porridge

SERVES 2

80g (¾ cup) rolled oats

400ml (generous 1½ cups)
sweetened almond milk

pinch of ground cinnamon

1 apple, grated

handful of sultanas
(golden raisins)

Everyone needs a good porridge recipe, for those mornings when only creamy, cooked oats will do. This version combines all of the flavours of apple pie, to take this comfort food to the next level. Use your favourite variety of seasonal apple, for subtle changes throughout the year.

1 Add the oats, almond milk and cinnamon to a pan and simmer over a medium-high heat for 4–5 minutes, stirring frequently.

2 Stir through the grated apple and sultanas and cook for a further 2–3 minutes until the apple begins to soften.

3 Serve in bowls and enjoy immediately.

EASY TIP

This porridge has enough flavour and sweetness from the apple, spices and sultanas to forgo a topping, but if you can't resist a little something, sprinkle with a little brown sugar.

Baked bananas and pineapple with coconut yogurt and walnuts

SERVES 4

4 bananas, peeled and sliced in half lengthways

1 pineapple, peeled and sliced into large chunks, tough core discarded

handful of sultanas (golden raisins)

pinch of ground cinnamon

4 tbsp coconut yogurt

2 tbsp roughly chopped walnuts

Sweet, juicy tropical fruits and plump sultanas (golden raisins) are baked before topping with cooling coconut yogurt and walnuts. Not exclusive to breakfast time, this also makes a delicious hot dessert.

1 Preheat the oven to 180°C/350°F/gas mark 4.

2 Arrange the bananas, pineapple and sultanas in a deep baking dish, then sprinkle with cinnamon. Loosely cover with foil, then bake in the oven for 35–40 minutes until the bananas have browned slightly and the pineapple is soft and juicy.

3 Remove from the oven and spoon into four bowls. Top each one with a tablespoon of coconut yogurt and sprinkle with walnuts.

EASY TIP
This baked breakfast is a great way to use up any brown bananas.

Sticky griddled oranges with toasted almonds

SERVES 2

2 large unwaxed oranges, peeled and cut into 1cm (½in) thick slices

1 tbsp maple syrup

2 rounded tbsp flaked (slivered) almonds

4 tbsp chilled almond yogurt

Hot, sweet oranges are topped with cooling almond yogurt and crunchy toasted almonds in this light but full-of-flavour breakfast. Stack the orange slices high and feel free to increase the quantity of yogurt, if you like.

1 Heat a griddle pan over a medium-high heat.

2 Meanwhile, use a pastry brush to sweep both sides of the orange slices with maple syrup. Use tongs to place the orange slices onto the hot griddle pan in batches; cook for 1–2 minutes on each side until slightly charred.

3 Carefully remove from the pan and place on serving plates. Sprinkle the almonds onto the sticky griddle pan and toast for 2 minutes until golden.

4 Spoon the yogurt over the orange slices, then sprinkle with the toasted almonds.

EASY TIP

If you don't have almond yogurt available, simple soya or coconut yogurt make excellent alternatives.

Banana pancakes

SERVES 4

Suitable for freezing

1 medium-sized ripe banana, peeled

100g (1 cup) rolled oats

pinch of ground cinnamon

300ml (1¼ cups) sweetened soya milk

1 tbsp sunflower oil

generous drizzle of maple syrup

I love these fluffy banana pancakes as a sweet start to a lazy day. Use up that browning banana lurking in the fruit bowl, for a no-waste breakfast.

1 Throw the banana, oats, cinnamon and soya milk into a jug blender (or add the ingredients to a bowl and use a hand blender). Blitz into a semi-smooth batter.

2 Heat the oil in a frying pan over a low-medium heat.

3 Add tablespoon-sized amounts of the batter to the hot pan. Cook for 2 minutes until golden, then flip to the other side and cook for a further 2 minutes.

4 Pile up on serving plates and drizzle with maple syrup just before serving.

EASY TIP

Load with toppings of your choice! My favourites include, raspberries and blueberries, dark chocolate shavings, and even vegan whipped cream (available in large supermarkets).

Infused morning water

SERVES 4

handful of ice cubes

½ unwaxed grapefruit, thickly sliced

½ unwaxed orange, thickly sliced

½ unwaxed lemon, thickly sliced

handful of fresh mint leaves

Start your day hydrated! This jug of infused water looks tempting on the table, served with either sweet or savoury breakfast options.

1 Add the ice cubes to a 1-litre (4-cup) capacity jug, then throw in the sliced grapefruit, orange and lemon and mint leaves.

2 Pour in 1 litre (4 cups) tap, filtered or mineral water. Allow to infuse for a few minutes before drinking.

EASY TIP
Prepare the fruit and water the evening before, then refrigerate, for extra infusion time. Throw in the ice cubes before serving.

Berry breakfast crumble

SERVES 4

150g (1½ cups) blueberries

150g (1¼ cups) raspberries

150g (1¼ cups) blackberries

4 tbsp fresh orange juice

8 tbsp rolled oats

4 tbsp almonds, roughly chopped

1 tbsp pumpkin seeds

There's always time for dessert – especially for breakfast! This no-added-sugar bake is fruity and fresh, with a toasted oat, nut and pumpkin seed topping. Serve hot with a spoonful of creamy soya yogurt.

1 Preheat the oven to 200°C/400°F/gas mark 6.

2 Put the blueberries, raspberries and blackberries into a small roasting tray and spoon over the orange juice. Cover loosely with foil then bake in the oven for 20 minutes until the fruit has softened.

3 Evenly arrange the oats, almonds and pumpkin seeds on a baking tray. Toast in the oven for 5–7 minutes until golden.

4 Remove both trays from the oven. Scatter the oat topping over the fruit, then serve hot.

EASY TIP

Frozen berries work well instead of fresh fruits, if that is what you have available. Simply defrost before use.

POT · POT · POT · POT
1

Chocolate and cherry overnight oats

SERVES 1

50g (½ cup) rolled oats

100ml (scant ½ cup) chocolate soya milk

1 rounded tbsp unsweetened soya yogurt

handful of fresh cherries, pitted and halved

Prepare these overnight oats in the evening and enjoy a creamy and fuss-free breakfast in the morning. I love the flavours of chocolate and cherry, with a spoonful of sharper, unsweetened yogurt. These little pots will last in the fridge for up to 3 days, in sealed jars.

1 Add the oats and chocolate soya milk to a jar or bowl and stir together. Refrigerate overnight.

2 In the morning, stir and loosen with a little extra chocolate soya milk, if you like. Spoon over the yogurt and top with the cherries.

EASY TIP
Chocolate soya milk can be found in many supermarkets, both fresh in the chiller cabinet or ultra-heat treated (UHT) in the free-from aisle.

Pomegranate, orange and pistachio parfait

SERVES 2

1 unwaxed orange, peeled and thinly sliced into rounds

seeds of 1 pomegranate

8 tbsp vanilla soya yogurt

2 tbsp shelled pistachios, chopped

4 mint leaves, finely chopped

For a light yet impressive breakfast, treat yourself to a parfait, jewelled with pomegranate and vibrant orange. The mint and pistachio topping adds that all important freshness and crunch.

1 In two small serving glasses, arrange layers of orange slices, pomegranate seeds and yogurt, finishing with a layer of yogurt at the top of the glass.

2 Scatter with chopped pistachios and mint just before serving.

EASY TIP

If you're short of time, you can buy packs of pomegranate seeds in large supermarkets; this will save you the effort of removing the juicy seeds of the fruit. However, if you're using a whole pomegranate, simply slice the fruit in half with the seeds facing downwards over a bowl, then whack with a wooden spoon for easy removal.

Baked oat breakfast cups

MAKES 6

½ tsp sunflower oil

1 ripe banana, peeled

2 tbsp maple syrup

pinch of ground cinnamon

100g (1 cup) rolled oats

6 tbsp vanilla soya yogurt

6 pieces of small soft fruits, such as blueberries, blackberries, strawberries, pear slices, peach slices

Who else loves a breakfast that looks like patisserie? Personalize these cute baked oat cups with your favourite non-dairy yogurt and fruits for a satisfying breakfast that everyone will love.

1 Preheat the oven to 180°C/350°F/gas mark 4, then use a pastry brush to grease six holes of a muffin tray.

2 In a bowl, mash the banana with a fork until semi-smooth. Add the maple syrup, cinnamon and oats, then stir until combined.

3 Take tablespoon-sized amounts of the mixture and press into the tin, following the shape of each individual cavity, so you form a hollow shell. Bake in the oven for 20–25 minutes until golden and crisp at the edges.

4 Remove from the oven and allow to stand for a few moments before using a teaspoon to lift the oat cups out of the tin.

5 Fill each oat cup with soya yogurt, before placing a small piece of fruit on top.

EASY TIP

Prepare these cups the day before and store in a sealed container, then simply fill with yogurt and fruit just before serving.

Chocolate, orange and almond pastries

MAKES ABOUT 10

1 sheet of ready rolled puff pastry (ensure dairy-free)

200g (7oz) vegan chocolate spread

2 tbsp (slivered) flaked almonds

zest of 1 unwaxed orange

Nothing beats a chocolate-filled pastry and a hot coffee to start the day. These pastry swirls are quick to prepare and bake, and delicious to eat.

1 Preheat the oven to 220°C/425°F/gas mark 7 and line two baking sheets with baking parchment.

2 Unroll the puff pastry and spoon over the chocolate spread. Smooth it liberally over one whole side the pastry, then scatter over the almonds and orange zest.

3 Starting at one end of the pastry, tightly roll the pastry to the other side, to form a full roll. Slice the roll into 10 pieces and lay them flat on the baking tray.

4 Bake the swirls in the oven for 12–15 minutes until the pastry is golden. Serve hot or cold.

EASY TIP

Many brands of ready-rolled puff pastry are vegan, as oil is often used rather than butter. Remove the pastry from your fridge about 30 minutes before using, to avoid any cracks in the breakfast pastries.

PB&J breakfast cookies

MAKES 8

---

6 rounded tbsp smooth peanut butter

4 tbsp rolled oats

4 tbsp roasted peanuts, roughly chopped

4 tbsp soya milk

8 tsp strawberry jam

Loved by kids and adults alike, these little breakfast cookies have an all-American flavour of peanut butter and strawberry jam. Enjoy warm, with a glass of ice-cold soya milk.

1 Preheat the oven to 200°C/400°F/gas mark 6 and line a baking tray with baking parchment.

2 In a large bowl, stir together the peanut butter, oats and peanuts. Spoon in the soya milk gradually, stirring to form a thick dough.

3 Separate the dough into eight even pieces. Roll into balls then place on the baking tray. Flatten slightly with your thumb, leaving a thumbprint visible in the top. Dollop a teaspoon of jam into each thumbprint.

4 Bake in the oven for 10–12 minutes until golden around the edges. Best enjoyed warm.

EASY TIP

The oil content of peanut butter varies from brand to brand, so adjust the amount of soya milk used for the dough. The uncooked dough should be stiff and easy to shape.

Microwave blueberry muffin

SERVES 1

4 tbsp self-raising flour

2 tbsp granulated sugar

handful of blueberries

4 tbsp soya milk

1 tbsp sunflower oil

1 tsp good-quality vanilla extract

For those mornings when you need all the sweet satisfaction of a blueberry muffin, but don't have the time to cook up a batch, throw together these store cupboard ingredients and cook in the microwave. The timing is based on a standard 850W microwave.

1 Mix together the flour and sugar in a large mug, then stir in the blueberries.

2 Spoon in the soya milk, sunflower oil and vanilla extract, then mix until smooth.

3 Microwave for 1 minute 30 seconds. Allow to cool for 2 minutes before enjoying.

EASY TIP

For a warming twist, add a pinch of cinnamon to the batter before cooking. For a summery version, finely grate a little unwaxed lemon zest into the mix.

MINUTE · MINUTE · 15

Pretzel, peanut butter and banana bagels

SERVES 4

4 cinnamon bagels (ensure vegan)

4 tbsp smooth peanut butter

8 snack-sized salted pretzels, roughly chopped

1 banana, peeled and thinly sliced

1 square of dark chocolate (ensure vegan), grated

Bored with the same old bagel toppings? Add an unexpected crunch with pretzels – salted pretzels will enhance the flavour of peanut butter and chocolate, making these bagels the perfect weekend treat! So, what are you waiting for?

1 Split the bagels in half, then toast in batches until each bagel half is golden and hot.

2 Smooth an even layer of peanut butter over each bagel half, then press over the chopped salted pretzels.

3 Lay over slices of banana, then scatter with grated dark chocolate. Serve warm.

EASY TIP

Experiment with different flavours of bagel, including original, raisin or sesame.

Cream cheese and blueberry toast

SERVES 4

150g (1½ cups) blueberries

2 tbsp maple syrup

pinch of ground cinnamon

zest and juice of 1 unwaxed lemon

4 thick slices of white sourdough bread

2 tbsp vegan mild cream cheese

This creamy and fruity toast reminds me of eating cheesecake – and what better time to have it than breakfast?! If you don't have fresh blueberries to hand, frozen blueberries are a great substitute.

1 Add the blueberries, maple syrup and cinnamon to a pan, then place over a medium heat for 4–5 minutes, stirring and breaking down the blueberries with a wooden spoon. Stir in the lemon zest and juice and cook for a further 2 minutes.

2 Meanwhile, toast the bread slices until golden and crisp, then spread generously with the vegan cream cheese.

3 Place the toasts on serving plates, then spoon over the blueberry compote. Serve hot.

EASY TIP

You'll find many brands and flavours of vegan cream cheese in large supermarkets; for this recipe, opt for a mild cream cheese without any additional flavours.

Chai French toast

SERVES 4

200ml (generous ¾ cup) sweetened soya milk

2 tbsp maple syrup

1 tsp good-quality vanilla extract

100g (scant 1 cup) plain (all-purpose) flour

1 tsp ground cinnamon

generous pinch of grated nutmeg

generous pinch of ground cardamom

generous pinch of ground cloves

4 tbsp sunflower oil

4 thick slices of white bread, halved diagonally

1 tsp granulated sugar

Start your weekend with some sweet spice, beautifully incorporated into classic French toast. Brew up a cafetière of coffee, relax with the newspaper and savour this special breakfast.

1 Whisk together the soya milk, maple syrup and vanilla extract in a large bowl. Stir in the flour, cinnamon, nutmeg, cardamom and cloves and whisk until smooth and thick.

2 Heat half the sunflower oil in a frying pan while you dip the bread fully in the batter, coating both sides. Use tongs to place the bread into the pan, cooking in batches for 2–3 minutes on each side until golden and crisp and adding the remaining oil to the pan between batches.

3 Carefully remove from the pan and drain on kitchen paper for a couple of minutes. Sprinkle sugar over the slices before serving hot.

EASY TIP

To save time in the morning, make the batter the evening before and keep in the fridge. It may thicken in this time, so whisk in a tablespoon of soya milk before dipping the bread.

Breakfast bruschetta

SERVES 2

1 small baguette (French stick), diagonally sliced into 6 even pieces

1 large avocado, peeled, stoned and roughly diced

10 cherry tomatoes, roughly chopped

handful of fresh chives, finely chopped

generous drizzle of good-quality extra virgin olive oil

generous pinch each of sea salt and black pepper

If you love a savoury breakfast, this fast and full-of-flavour bruschetta will hit the spot. Choose a firm avocado to dice, and fragrant cherry tomatoes brought to room temperature to get the best out of these ingredients.

1 Heat up a griddle pan over a medium-high heat, then carefully lay the slices of bread in the pan. Toast for 3–4 minutes until nicely golden with grill lines.

2 Meanwhile, in a bowl, stir together the avocado, tomatoes, chives and olive oil. Season to taste with salt and pepper.

3 Use tongs to remove the toasted bread from the griddle pan, then place on serving plates. Spoon the avocado mix generously onto the slices, then serve immediately.

EASY TIP
If you don't have fresh chives available, substitute for finely chopped spring onion (scallion) tops.

Creamy garlic mushrooms

SERVES 2

1 tbsp sunflower oil

200g (3 cups) button mushrooms

1 garlic clove, peeled and crushed

250ml (1 cup) soya single (light) cream

small handful of dill, finely chopped

generous pinch each of sea salt and black pepper

Who can say no to a dish of creamy, garlicky mushrooms? Divine, earthy and fragrant, this easy-to-prepare dish makes for a decadent brunch. Serve simply with toast, or with colcannon hash browns (page 66).

1 Heat the oil in a large pan, add the mushrooms and cook over a medium-high heat for 4–5 minutes until fragrant, stirring frequently. Stir in the garlic and cook for a further minute.

2 Pour in the soya cream and reduce the heat to medium. Simmer for 10 minutes to allow the cream to reduce down.

3 Remove from the heat and stir through the dill. Season to taste with sea salt and black pepper. Serve hot.

EASY TIP

You'll find soya single cream readily available in supermarkets. Soya cream has a luxurious texture and neutral flavour, perfect for pairing with earthy mushrooms and fresh dill.

Toasted muffins with harissa yogurt, asparagus and spinach

SERVES 4

125g (4oz) asparagus spears, tough ends discarded

4 handfuls of baby spinach leaves, tough stems discarded

4 plain English muffins, split into two halves

4 tbsp unsweetened plain soya yogurt

2 tsp harissa paste

drizzle of good-quality extra virgin olive oil

generous pinch each of sea salt and black pepper

Treat yourself to a little taste of luxury for breakfast or brunch. Lightly toasted muffins are topped with spinach, spiced yogurt and asparagus spears, before being drizzled with extra virgin olive oil. Perfect to share with friends and family.

1 Bring a large pan of water to the boil, then add the asparagus and cook for 4–5 minutes. Throw in the spinach for 1 minute, then drain and keep warm.

2 Meanwhile, toast the muffin halves until golden.

3 Put in the soya yogurt into a bowl and season to taste with sea salt. Lightly swirl in the harissa paste.

4 Lay the muffin halves on serving plates and evenly spoon over the spinach. Add a spoonful of harissa yogurt on top of the spinach. Top with the asparagus spears, then drizzle over a little olive oil. Season generously with black pepper and serve warm.

EASY TIP

Asparagus is most affordable when in season, which is also when it has the best flavour and texture.

Tomato and red onion frittatas

MAKES 6

½ tsp sunflower oil

280g (9oz) block of extra-firm tofu, drained of excess moisture (no need to press)

½ tsp ground turmeric

1 tsp dried oregano

1 tbsp soya milk

¼ red onion, thinly sliced

6 sundried tomatoes in oil, drained and roughly sliced

generous pinch each of sea salt and black pepper

No eggs, no problem! These mini frittatas are perfect for brunch (or lunch) and can be made the night before and kept in the fridge, to be enjoyed either reheated or cold. I love the flavours of sundried tomatoes, oregano and red onion in these fluffy frittatas!

1 Preheat the oven to 200°C/400°F/gas mark 6. Brush six holes of a muffin tray with a little sunflower oil.

2 Break the tofu up into a high-powered jug blender or food processor, then spoon in the turmeric, oregano and soya milk. Add 3 tablespoons cold water and blitz on high speed, then add another 3 tablespoons cold water and blitz again to form a thick paste (it should be thick enough to spoon rather than pour). Season with sea salt and plenty of black pepper.

3 Stir in the sliced red onion and sundried tomatoes.

4 Spoon 2 tablespoons of the mix into each hole of the muffin tray, ensuring an even distribution of onion and tomato.

5 Bake in the oven for 15 minutes, then reduce the heat to 180°C/350°F/gas mark 4 and bake for a further 5–7 minutes until the frittatas appear set. Remove from the oven and allow to stand for a few minutes before removing from the tray.

EASY TIP

Mix up the flavours by substituting tomatoes and red onion for asparagus and spinach, cooked potato and spring onion (scallion) or broccoli and green beans.

Mexican scrambled tofu

SERVES 4

280g (9oz) block of extra-firm tofu

1 tbsp sunflower oil

1 red onion, sliced into thin rings

1 red (bell) pepper, deseeded and finely chopped

handful of frozen sweetcorn

1 rounded tsp mild chilli powder

1 tsp ground turmeric

1 x 400g (14oz) can of red kidney beans, drained and rinsed

2 spring onions (scallions), finely chopped

handful of coriander (cilantro) leaves

1 small red chilli, deseeded and thinly sliced into rounds

1 avocado, peeled, stoned and thinly sliced

4 thick slices of sourdough bread

generous pinch each of smoked sea salt and black pepper

How do you like your tofu in the morning? This Mexican-inspired version has a little spice to set you up for the day ahead. Serve this easy brunch scramble family-style, taking the pan to the table for everyone to help themselves. Delicious served with thick slices of toasted sourdough.

1 Lay the block of tofu on a piece of kitchen paper or a clean tea towel, and allow to drain for 10 minutes. Crumble the tofu into a bowl and use a fork to separate the larger pieces until the texture resembles that of scrambled eggs. Set aside.

2 Heat the oil in a large frying pan, add the red onion, pepper and sweetcorn and cook over a medium heat for 3–4 minutes until the onion begins to soften.

3 Stir in the chilli powder and turmeric, along with 3 tablespoons cold water. Stir in the crumbled tofu and gently mix until it is fully coated in the spice mixture.

4 Pour in the kidney beans, then simmer for 8–10 minutes, stirring occasionally.

5 Remove the pan from the heat and scatter over the spring onions (scallions), coriander (cilantro) and red chilli. Lay the avocado slices over, then season with smoked sea salt and black pepper.

6 Toast the sourdough until golden, then serve with the scramble.

EASY TIP

If you're new to cooking tofu, this is the perfect recipe for you to enjoy, as the tofu requires no pressing.

5 INGREDIENTS

Roasted tomatoes on toast

SERVES 2

300g (2 cups) cherry tomatoes

pinch of finely chopped fresh rosemary

drizzle of olive oil

2 thick slices of sourdough bread

generous pinch each of sea salt and black pepper

Simple is often best, especially when it comes to breakfast. Choose ripe, sweet cherry tomatoes and roast with rosemary and a drizzle of olive oil. Serve over freshly toasted sourdough, for a tangy contrast to the sweet tomatoes.

1 Preheat the oven to 180°C/350°F/gas mark 4.

2 Arrange the tomatoes on a baking tray and sprinkle with the rosemary. Drizzle with olive oil then roast in the oven for 25–30 minutes until the skins have slightly browned and blistered.

3 Meanwhile, toast the sourdough until lightly golden.

4 Remove the tomatoes from the oven and scatter with sea salt and black pepper. Spoon the tomatoes over the toast and serve hot.

EASY TIP
Save any leftover roasted tomatoes to stir through pasta, or enjoy chilled with antipasti.

Sweet potato, pepper and red bean hash

SERVES 2 GENEROUSLY

1 tbsp sunflower oil

2 sweet potatoes, peeled and chopped into 2cm (1in) cubes

1 red onion, thinly sliced

1 yellow (bell) pepper, deseeded and thinly sliced

1 x 400g (14oz) can of red kidney beans, drained and rinsed

1 tsp mild chilli powder

1 tsp smoked paprika

juice of 1 unwaxed lime

few drops of Tabasco

generous handful of flat-leaf parsley, finely chopped

generous pinch each of smoked sea salt and black pepper

Whip up a hearty brunch that everyone will love, with smoky flavours, lime juice and a kick of Tabasco! Serve with vegan sour cream or a spoonful of unsweetened soya yogurt.

1 Heat the oil in a large frying pan and throw in the sweet potatoes. Cook over a medium-high heat for 10 minutes, stirring frequently to avoid sticking.

2 Add the red onion and pepper and cook for a further 10 minutes, stirring frequently.

3 When the sweet potato has softened, stir in the kidney beans, chilli powder and smoked paprika and cook for a 2–3 minutes, coating all of the ingredients in the spices.

4 Remove from the heat and squeeze over the lime juice. Sprinkle over a few drops of Tabasco to taste and scatter with the chopped parsley. Season generously with smoked sea salt and black pepper just before serving.

EASY TIP

Chop the sweet potatoes, red onion and pepper up to a day in advance, then simply throw in the pan for a fuss-free brunch.

Brunch butterbean masala

SERVES 2 GENEROUSLY

Suitable for freezing

1 tbsp sunflower oil

1 onion, finely chopped

1 garlic clove, crushed

2 tsp garam masala

1 tsp ground cumin

pinch of dried chilli flakes

1 x 400g (14oz) can of chopped tomatoes

1 x 400g (14oz) can of butterbeans, drained and rinsed

1 tbsp mango chutney

1 tbsp coconut yogurt

generous handful of coriander (cilantro), roughly chopped

generous pinch of sea salt

When it's too late for breakfast, but too early for lunch, make time for this gently spiced butterbean masala, with mango chutney, cumin and coconut yogurt. It's delicate enough for brunch, with just a hint of chilli to awaken your senses. Serve with toast for dipping, or simply eat with a spoon.

1 Heat the oil in a large pan and add the onion. Cook over a medium heat for 4–5 minutes, stirring frequently until the onion begins to turn golden. Stir in the garlic, garam masala, cumin and chilli flakes and cook for a further minute.

2 Pour in the chopped tomatoes and butterbeans, then simmer over a low-medium heat for 20 minutes, stirring occasionally.

3 Remove from the heat and stir through the mango chutney and coconut yogurt. Scatter over the coriander (cilantro) and season to taste with sea salt. Serve hot.

EASY TIP

This masala can be frozen for up to 3 months. Spoon into freezer-safe containers before you add the yogurt and coriander, then add these ingredients in fresh when you reheat the masala.

Smoky shakshuka

SERVES 2 GENEROUSLY

Suitable for freezing (before adding the yogurt)

1 tbsp sunflower oil

1 onion, finely chopped

1 red (bell) pepper, deseeded and thinly sliced

2 garlic cloves, crushed

1 x 400g (14oz) can of chopped tomatoes

1 x 400g (14oz) can of chickpeas (garbanzo beans), drained and rinsed

1 tsp harissa paste

generous handful of flat-leaf parsley, roughly chopped

generous handful of coriander (cilantro), roughly chopped

small handful of dill, roughly chopped

2 rounded tbsp unsweetened soya yogurt

pinch of smoked paprika

½ unwaxed lemon, cut into wedges, to serve

generous pinch each of smoked sea salt and black pepper

Vegans don't need to miss out on the brunch fun! This gently spiced bowl food has fresh bursts of herbs, before being topped with paprika yogurt. Serve with soldiers of toasted pitta or sourdough, drizzled with a little extra virgin olive oil.

1 Heat the oil in a large pan, add the onion and pepper and cook over a medium heat for 4–5 minutes, stirring occasionally, until the onion begins to turn golden. Stir in the garlic and cook for a further minute.

2 Pour in the chopped tomatoes, chickpeas and harissa paste, then simmer for 20 minutes, stirring frequently.

3 Remove from the heat and stir through the parsley, coriander and dill, reserving some for serving. Season to taste with smoked sea salt and black pepper.

4 Ladle into serving dishes and spoon over a tablespoon of soya yogurt in each bowlful. Sprinkle a little smoked paprika over the yogurt, then scatter with the remaining herbs and serve with the lemon wedges.

EASY TIP

Cut up the onion, pepper, herbs and lemon in advance, then refrigerate for up to 12 hours before using.

Store cupboard kedgeree

SERVES 4

1 tbsp sunflower oil

1 onion, finely chopped

1 garlic clove, crushed

1 tsp mild curry powder

½ tsp ground turmeric

½ tsp ground cumin

150g (¾ cup) basmati rice

700ml (2¾ cups) hot water

100g (⅔ cup) jarred chargrilled artichokes in oil, drained and roughly chopped

8 green beans, halved

2 tbsp frozen peas

generous handful of fresh dill, finely chopped

juice of ½ unwaxed lemon

pinch each of fine sea salt and black pepper

Perfect for breakfast or brunch, this gently spiced dish can be served at the table in the cooking pot, for everyone to help themselves. Basmati rice ensures this dish is ready quickly, for when you need something warming and filling to start the day.

1 Heat the sunflower oil in a large pan, add the onion and garlic and cook over a medium-high heat for 2 minutes. Spoon in the curry powder, turmeric and cumin and cook for 1 further minute.

2 Stir through the rice and pour in 500ml (2 cups) of the water. Simmer for 5 minutes, stirring frequently.

3 Add the artichokes and green beans and pour in the remaining 200ml (¾ cup) water. Cook for a further 4 minutes until the water has absorbed into the rice. Then stir through the peas and cook for a further minute.

4 Once the rice is cooked, remove from the heat and stir through the dill. Squeeze over the lemon juice and season to taste with salt and pepper. Serve hot.

EASY TIP

You'll find jarred chargrilled artichokes readily available in supermarkets. Use this versatile ingredient on homemade pizzas, as part of a mezze board, or in a simple salad.

Slow cooker breakfast burritos

SERVES 4

*Suitable for freezing
(filling only)*

2 sweet potatoes, peeled and evenly chopped into 2cm (¾in) chunks

1 onion, thickly sliced

1 red (bell) pepper, deseeded and thickly sliced

200g (7oz) canned or frozen sweetcorn

1 x 400g (14oz) can of chopped tomatoes

1 x 400g (14oz) can of red kidney beans, drained and rinsed

2 tsp mild chilli powder

1 tsp smoked paprika

1 tsp ground cinnamon

4 tbsp basmati rice

handful of coriander (cilantro), roughly chopped

4 large white tortilla wraps

1 avocado, peeled, stoned and sliced

generous pinch of smoked sea salt

Don't just dream about waking up to burritos, set your slow cooker to do the hard work while you sleep! All you'll have to do on waking is to wrap the spicy filling in tortilla wraps with avocado slices – then enjoy at home, or on the go.

1 Set the slow cooker to low and preheat.

2 Add the sweet potato, onion, red pepper, sweetcorn, chopped tomatoes, kidney beans, chilli powder, smoked paprika and ground cinnamon to the slow cooker.

3 Stir in the rice with 100ml (scant ½ cup) cold water, then place the lid on the slow cooker. Cook on low for 6–7 hours until the sweet potato has softened and the rice is cooked. Season to taste with smoked sea salt, then stir in the coriander.

4 Lay out the tortilla wraps on four separate pieces of foil. Divide the avocado slices between them, then spoon in the slow-cooked filling. Tightly wrap the tortillas with the foil around them and serve hot.

EASY TIP

Don't be tempted to add any more liquid to the slow cooker during cooking, as less liquid is evaporated compared to cooking on the hob. You want the filling to be a little starchy for the perfect burrito filling.

Colcannon hash browns

MAKES 4

1 large baking potato, scrubbed clean

2 leaves of savoy cabbage, kale or cavolo nero, finely chopped

2 spring onions (scallions), finely chopped

2 tbsp sunflower oil

generous pinch each of sea salt and black pepper

If you thought hash browns couldn't get any better, think again! This version combines all the flavours of classic colcannon mashed potatoes, but as a breakfast-friendly dish. Cook until golden and crisp on the outside, then serve as part of a vegan full English breakfast, with a glug of tomato ketchup.

1 Grate the potato onto a clean, dry tea towel or cloth, then squeeze out as much moisture as possible. When no more moisture can be squeezed out, tip the grated potato into a bowl.

2 Stir the cabbage and spring onions through the potato and season generously with sea salt and black pepper.

3 Firmly shape hash brown rounds in your hands using 2 tablespoons of the mix at a time, or press into a scone cutter for a neater finish.

4 Heat the sunflower oil in a frying pan, then carefully add the hash browns. Cook for 4–5 minutes, using a spatula to gently press down on each hash brown. Turn each over and cook the other side for 4–5 minutes until golden. Serve hot.

EASY TIP

There's no need to peel the potato before grating it, simply scrub it thoroughly before use. This will save you time and give the hash browns a rustic look!

Breakfast pizzas

SERVES 2

---

1 tbsp olive oil

8 closed-cup mushrooms, brushed clean and sliced

8 cherry tomatoes

generous handful of spinach leaves

2 large white pitta breads

few drops of Tabasco

generous pinch each of sea salt and black pepper

It's never too early for pizza, but if you don't quite believe me, whip up these breakfast-friendly versions, with a toasted pitta base, mushrooms, tomatoes and spinach. Don't forget that all-important sprinkle of Tabasco, to really wake you up.

1 Heat the oil in a pan, add the mushrooms and tomatoes and cook over a medium heat for 4–5 minutes until fragrant. Throw in the spinach and cook down for a further 2 minutes, stirring occasionally.

2 Meanwhile, toast the pitta breads until golden and crisp.

3 Lay the toasted pitta breads on serving plates and spoon over the cooked mushrooms, tomatoes and spinach. Sprinkle over a few drops of Tabasco, then season with sea salt and black pepper. Serve hot.

EASY TIP

Pitta breads freeze well and defrost in no time, so keep some in the freezer for easy snacking, at any time of the day.

POT · POT · POT · POT · 1

Baked full English breakfast

SERVES 2

6 new potatoes, halved

10 closed-cup mushrooms, brushed clean and sliced

10 baby plum tomatoes

1 slice of day-old bread, roughly chopped into cubes

sunflower oil, for drizzling

1 x 200g (7oz) can of baked beans

1 avocado, peeled, stoned and sliced

generous pinch each of sea salt and black pepper

Fancy a fry-up but don't fancy all the messy washing up? This full breakfast is cooked in just one roasting tin, leaving you time to get on with better things while the oven works its magic.

1 Preheat the oven to 180°C/350°F/gas mark 4.

2 Neatly arrange the potatoes, mushrooms, tomatoes and bread in a deep roasting tray, then drizzle with sunflower oil. Bake in the oven for 30 minutes until the potatoes begin to soften.

3 Remove from the oven and spoon in the baked beans, without adding too much of the sauce. Loosely cover with foil and return to the oven for 10 minutes.

4 Remove from the oven and season with salt and pepper. Serve with avocado slices.

EASY TIP

The smaller cans of baked beans are ideal to use for this breakfast, but if you fancy more, feel free to throw in a full sized (400g/14oz) can – just be sure to use a large enough roasting tin.

Bloody Mary

SERVES 2

100ml (scant ½ cup) vodka

500ml (2 cups) chilled tomato juice

few drops of Tabasco

few drops of Worcestershire sauce (ensure vegan)

pinch of sea salt

2 celery sticks, to serve

Take brunch to the next level with a glass of classic Bloody Mary. This vodka-infused morning cocktail is tangy and feisty, making it the perfect accompaniment to a baked full English breakfast (page 69), although it's equally as delicious without the vodka.

1 Pour the vodka and tomato juice into a jug, then stir in the Tabasco, Worcestershire sauce and sea salt and mix until combined.

2 Pour evenly between two chilled glasses and add the celery sticks to serve.

EASY TIP

Some brands of Worcestershire sauce contain anchovy (fish). There are vegan brands of Worcestershire sauce available in supermarkets, so be sure to always check before you buy.

MINUTE. MINUTE. 15

Frozen tropical smoothie

SERVES 2

generous handful of frozen mango chunks

1 banana, peeled

250ml (1 cup) pineapple juice, chilled

juice of 1 unwaxed lime

If you can't wake up to sunny skies and a sea view, blitz up this frozen smoothie to transport you to a tropical place, wherever you are. Using frozen mango keeps the smoothie cool and refreshing, while giving a deliciously thick texture.

1 Add the mango and banana to a high-powered jug blender, then pour in the pineapple juice and lime juice.

2 Blitz until completely smooth, then pour into glasses and serve immediately.

EASY TIP

Bags of frozen mango chunks can be found in large supermarkets, or simply chop a fresh mango into even chunks, then place in an even layer in a freezer-safe container. Freeze for up to 3 months for optimum freshness.

Lunch

INGREDIENTS 5

Quick beetroot, pear and Puy lentil salad

SERVES 2 GENEROUSLY

250g (3 cups) ready-to-eat Puy lentils, drained and rinsed

generous drizzle of good-quality extra virgin olive oil

small handful of fresh dill, finely chopped

pinch of black pepper

300g (10oz) vacuum-packed cooked beetroot (beet), drained and sliced

1 conference pear, thinly sliced

This simple five-minute salad is protein-packed, herby and perfect for autumn lunches. Puy lentils have a satisfying bite and nutty flavour, and the pre-cooked packs are great to keep in the cupboard for lazy lunches. Take the effort out of preparing and roasting whole beetroots by using prepared vacuum-packed beetroots, found in the chiller aisles of most supermarkets.

1 Tip the lentils into a serving dish and drizzle with olive oil. Stir through the dill and season with black pepper.

2 Roughly stir through the sliced beetroot and pear.

EASY TIP

This salad will last for up to 3 days in the fridge, making it perfect for preparing in advance.

Courgette caponata

SERVES 2

Suitable for freezing

1 tbsp sunflower oil

1 red onion, thinly sliced

2 medium courgettes (zucchini), roughly sliced into rounds

8 cherry tomatoes

2 tbsp balsamic vinegar

small handful of basil leaves

generous pinch each of sea salt and black pepper

I created this dish for a friend who hates aubergines (eggplants) and it was so delicious, I just had to share it with you. Traditionally, caponata is made with aubergines and served warm with breads, or chilled as antipasti. The sweetness of the tomatoes contrasts beautifully with the balsamic vinegar, to give a perfect sweet and sour flavour to the dish. Serve on toasted ciabatta, or stir through pasta.

1 Heat the oil in a large pan, add the red onion and courgettes and cook over a high heat for 5–6 minutes, stirring constantly to avoid burning. Add the tomatoes and cook for 2 further minutes.

2 Spoon in the balsamic vinegar and stir through. Reduce for 2–3 minutes.

3 Remove from the heat and scatter with basil leaves. Season to taste with salt and pepper.

EASY TIP

This is a great way to use up a seasonal glut of courgettes. The dish also freezes beautifully, so make a big batch and freeze in portions for another time.

Pasta e ceci

SERVES 4

Suitable for freezing

1 tbsp sunflower oil

1 onion, finely diced

1 x 400g (14oz) can of chopped tomatoes with herbs

1 x 400g (14oz) can of chickpeas (garbanzo beans), drained and rinsed

500ml (2 cups) hot vegetable stock

5 tbsp dried small soup pasta, such as margheritine (ensure egg-free)

generous pinch each of sea salt and black pepper

Pasta and chickpeas, Italian-style. If you've been lucky enough to visit Rome, you'll have seen *pasta e ceci*, a simple tomato-based soup which is delicious served with grilled vegan cheese toasts. In this five-ingredient version, I like to use good-quality canned chopped tomatoes with herbs (available in supermarkets), but if you only have simple canned chopped tomatoes in the store cupboard, just add in a teaspoonful of dried mixed herbs.

1 In a large pan, heat the oil and onion over a medium heat for 3–4 minutes until softened but not browned.

2 Pour in the chopped tomatoes, chickpeas and vegetable stock, then simmer for 10 minutes, stirring occasionally.

3 Add the pasta and cook for a further 8–10 minutes until *al dente*. Remove from the heat and season with plenty of salt and pepper.

EASY TIP

Add a sprig of fresh rosemary to the pan with the chopped tomatoes, then remove before serving, for an extra layer of flavour without much effort.

Lemon and pea rice salad

SERVES 2 GENEROUSLY

Suitable for freezing

1 tbsp sunflower oil

1 onion, finely diced

1 garlic clove, crushed

200g (1 cup) brown basmati rice

450ml (scant 2 cups) hot vegetable stock

pinch of ground turmeric

4 tbsp frozen peas

zest and juice of 1 unwaxed lemon

small handful of flat-leaf parsley, roughly chopped

small handful of mint leaves, roughly chopped

2 tbsp pine nuts

generous pinch each of sea salt and black pepper

Delicious hot or cold, this rice salad has a nutty flavour with pops of lemon, the sweet taste of peas, and summery herbs. Share this pilaf-style or refrigerate in sealed boxes for up to 2 days for portable lunches.

1 Heat the oil in a large pan, add the onion and cook over a high heat for 2–3 minutes until the onion has started to soften. Add the garlic and cook for 1 further minute.

2 Pour in the rice, vegetable stock and turmeric then reduce the heat to medium. Cook the rice for 15 minutes, stirring frequently to avoid sticking. Once cooked, remove from the heat, spoon in the frozen peas and place a lid over the pan, then allow it to stand for 10 minutes.

3 Stir through the lemon zest and juice and herbs. Scatter over the pine nuts and season with sea salt and plenty of black pepper.

EASY TIP

Brown basmati rice brings a deliciously nutty flavour to this dish. It takes a little longer to cook than white basmati rice, but it's worth the wait for the extra depth of flavour.

Carrot and coriander fritters

SERVES 2

120g (1 cup) plain (all-purpose) flour

2 tsp baking powder

½ tsp dried mixed herbs

½ tsp salt

1 medium carrot, peeled and grated

small handful of coriander (cilantro), finely chopped

4 tbsp sunflower oil

I love these quick and tasty fritters, which are perfect for using up any bendy carrots left at the back of your fridge. I love to throw in a handful of fresh coriander, but mix the flavours up by switching to fresh dill or flat-leaf parsley.

1 Mix the flour, baking powder, dried mixed herbs and salt together in a large bowl. Stir through the grated carrot and coriander.

2 Heat the oil in a frying pan over a low-medium heat.

3 Pour up to 100ml (scant ½ cup) water into the dry ingredients to form a thick batter. Drop tablespoon-sized amounts of the batter into the pan and cook for 2–3 minutes until golden, then use a flat spatula to flip them over to cook the other side for 2–3 minutes. Serve hot.

EASY TIP

Serve with mango chutney for dipping, or swirl over a little coconut yogurt for a cooling contrast.

Herby kofte in lettuce cups

SERVES 2 GENEROUSLY

Suitable for freezing (kofte only)

1 tbsp sunflower oil

1 onion, diced

1 tsp ground cumin

½ tsp dried oregano

1 tbsp shelled pistachios

300g (10oz) drained and rinsed jarred or canned chickpeas (garbanzo beans)

1 tbsp brown sauce

140g (¾ cup) dried apricots, finely chopped

4 baby gem lettuce leaves

drizzle of good-quality tahini

generous pinch of sea salt

These baked kofte are deliciously crisp on the outside and fluffy on the inside. Dried apricots and pistachios give a deliciously sweet flavour, while brown sauce delivers a hit of spicy tamarind flavour. Equally delicious served in warmed flatbreads.

1 Preheat the oven to 200°C/400°F/gas mark 6.

2 Heat the oil and onion in a pan over a high heat for 2 minutes until the onion begins to soften. Stir in the cumin, oregano and pistachios and cook for a further minute.

3 Transfer the cooked onion and pistachio mixture to a blender or food processor, along with any remaining oil from the pan. Add the chickpeas, brown sauce and sea salt, then blitz until a thick, semi-smooth paste is created. Stir through the dried apricots.

4 Scoop out small tablespoon-sized amounts of the mixture and roll into balls – you should get 8 balls. Place on a baking tray and bake in the oven for 20–25 minutes until golden.

5 Place in lettuce leaf cups, then drizzle to taste with tahini.

EASY TIP

Jarred chickpeas blend more easily than their canned varieties and can be found in supermarkets; however, they are more expensive. If you're using canned chickpeas, rinse and drain as usual, then stand them in boiling water for 5 minutes to help them soften.

Coronation chickpea naan toasties

SERVES 2 GENEROUSLY

1 x 400g (14oz) can of chickpeas (garbanzo beans), drained and rinsed

2 tbsp coconut yogurt

1 tbsp mango chutney

1 tsp mild curry powder

pinch of ground turmeric

1 spring onion (scallion), finely chopped

2 tsp sunflower oil

2 large vegan naan breads

small handful of coriander (cilantro), roughly torn

When a plain vegan cheese toastie just won't do, whip up some spiced coronation chickpeas and sandwich between dairy-free naan breads, then grill until golden. Lunch doesn't get much better than this. Dip into lime pickle for a flavour experience that you'll want to recreate every lunchtime.

1 Add the chickpeas to a bowl, then mash roughly using a fork. Spoon in the yogurt, mango chutney, curry powder, turmeric and spring onion, then allow to infuse for 15 minutes.

2 Heat a griddle pan and use a pastry brush to brush a little oil over one side of each naan.

3 Spread the coronation chickpeas over the non-oiled side of one naan bread and scatter on the coriander. Place the other naan over the top, with the oiled side visible. Carefully place the sandwich on the hot griddle pan for 3–4 minutes, then use tongs or a flat spatula to turn the sandwich over and cook for a further 3–4 minutes until griddle marks appear. Serve hot.

EASY TIP

Commercially produced naan breads can often contain dairy yogurt or ghee, but vegan versions are available in large supermarkets, so be sure to check the ingredients.

Creamy coconut noodles

SERVES 2

1 x 400ml (14fl oz) can of full-fat coconut milk

1 tbsp Thai red curry paste (ensure vegan)

1 carrot, peeled and grated

300g (10oz) ready-to-wok noodles (ensure egg-free)

4 sugarsnap peas, sliced lengthways

few drops of light soy sauce

generous handful of coriander (cilantro), roughly torn

unwaxed lime wedges, to serve

Creamy and rich with a hint of Thai spices, these easy noodles make the perfect comforting lunch. They are easily transported and reheated in a glass jar (reheat without the metal lid) or Tupperware for your very own instant noodle pot, when you crave it most.

1 Heat the coconut milk in a large pan until simmering, then stir in the curry paste and grated carrot.

2 Carefully separate the noodles, then add to the pan. Simmer for 10–15 minutes until softened, and the coconut broth has thickened.

3 Add the sugarsnap peas and soy sauce and cook for a further 2–3 minutes until the sugarsnaps are *al dente*.

4 Remove from the heat and scatter with coriander and lime wedges just before serving.

EASY TIP

Ready-to-wok noodles are found in the ambient section of supermarkets, and unlike their chilled counterparts, they are often egg-free, but always check the label before buying.

Banh mi with quick pickles

SERVES 4

1 carrot, peeled and sliced into ribbons using a vegetable peeler

6cm (2½in) piece of cucumber, thinly sliced into matchsticks

1 spring onion (scallion), thinly sliced

1 small red chilli, deseeded and very thinly sliced

4 tbsp apple cider vinegar

280g (9oz) block of extra-firm tofu, drained and pressed (see page 21)

1 tbsp sunflower oil

2 tbsp smooth peanut butter

2 tsp light soy sauce

1 tsp sesame seeds

4 individual crusty baguettes (French sticks), sliced open

small handful of coriander (cilantro), roughly torn

Banh mi are Vietnamese-style sandwiches, served hot with crispy tofu, savoury nutty spread and pickled vegetables. This version is easy to make at home, and is the perfect weekend lunch to enjoy with family and friends.

1 Put the carrot ribbons, cucumber, spring onion and chilli into a bowl and spoon over the cider vinegar. Allow to stand for at least 10 minutes to pickle.

2 Slice the pressed tofu into 3 horizontal slices, then cut each slice into triangles. Heat the sunflower oil in a frying pan over a medium-high heat, then add the tofu. Cook for 4–5 minutes until crisp and golden, then use tongs to turn the tofu triangles and cook for another 4 minutes on the other side.

3 Meanwhile, in a small bowl, mix together the peanut butter, soy sauce and sesame seeds. Spread generously into the baguettes.

4 Load the hot tofu into the baguettes, then spoon in the quick pickles. Sprinkle in the coriander, then serve hot.

EASY TIP

The quick pickles and peanut spread can be made up to 2 days in advance, so you can simply cook the tofu fresh and save yourself some time.

Red lentil, coconut and lime soup

SERVES 4

Suitable for freezing

200g (1 cup) red lentils, rinsed

1 litre (4 cups) hot vegetable stock

1 tbsp mild curry paste (ensure dairy-free)

pinch of dried chilli flakes

1 x 400ml (14fl oz) can of full-fat coconut milk

2 tbsp coconut yogurt

juice of 1 unwaxed lime

generous pinch of sea salt

Warming, comforting and cooked in one pan – what's not to love? This lightly spiced soup has become a favourite in my kitchen, as it's so simple to make with just store cupboard ingredients.

1 Add the red lentils and vegetable stock to a large pan, then stir in the curry paste and dried chilli flakes. Bring to the boil, then simmer for 30 minutes over a low-medium heat, stirring frequently, until the lentils have broken down.

2 Pour in the coconut milk and cook for a further 10 minutes.

3 Remove from the heat and stir in the coconut yogurt, lime juice and sea salt. Serve hot.

EASY TIP
Switch up the mild curry paste for Thai green curry paste (ensure vegan) for a subtle change without any extra effort.

Sticky pulled jackfruit sandwiches

SERVES 2

*Suitable for freezing
(filling only)*

1 tbsp sunflower oil

1 onion, thinly sliced

1 tsp soft light brown sugar

1 x 400g (14oz) can of jackfruit,
thoroughly drained and rinsed,
then broken into strands

4 rounded tbsp barbecue sauce
(ensure vegan)

2 large white bread buns, sliced
in half

**Sticky, smoky and mouth-watering, these sandwiches
take the hassle out of pulled jackfruit. Caramelized
onions and brown sugar create the perfect base for
shredded jackfruit. Most brands of shop-bought
barbecue sauce is vegan-friendly, but always check the
label before buying. Load in tangy coleslaw (page 279)
for added crunch!**

1 Heat the oil and onion in a large frying pan and cook
over a medium heat for 5–6 minutes until it begins to
brown. Sprinkle in the brown sugar and cook for a further
2–3 minutes, stirring constantly to avoid sticking.

2 Stir in the jackfruit strands and barbecue sauce, then
cook for 5 minutes until the sauce begins to thicken and
become sticky. Stir frequently.

3 Meanwhile, lightly toast the bread buns until just
golden.

4 Generously spoon the sticky jackfruit onto the bottom
half of each bread bun, then place the top half over.

EASY TIP

Toast the bread buns by placing them flat side down on a
griddle (grill) pan, or oven-grill (broil) for 1–2 minutes until
lightly golden.

Satay salad

SERVES 1 GENEROUSLY

1 tbsp smooth peanut butter

1 tbsp light soy sauce

pinch of dried chilli flakes

generous handful of watercress

1 carrot, peeled and sliced into ribbons using a vegetable peeler

handful of sugarsnap peas, sliced diagonally

juice of ½ unwaxed lime

1 spring onion (scallion), finely sliced

small handful of coriander (cilantro), roughly chopped

1 tbsp roasted and salted peanuts, roughly chopped

Crunchy, fresh and zingy, with an addictively creamy peanut sauce, this salad delivers a flavour hit to satisfy any grumbly tummy. Don't forgo the final topping of spring onions, coriander and crushed peanuts to lift this salad to another level.

1 Mix together the peanut butter and soy sauce in a bowl with 3 tablespoons boiling water to create a creamy sauce. Stir in the chilli flakes and set aside.

2 Toss together the watercress, carrot and sugarsnap peas, then stir through the lime juice. Arrange on a serving plate, then drizzle over the satay sauce.

3 Sprinkle over the spring onion, coriander and peanuts and serve fresh.

EASY TIP

The salad is delicious with the warm, satay dressing, but it also tastes delicious chilled. Due to the varying oil content in each brand of peanut butter, you may need to add a little extra boiling water, as it will thicken as it cools.

Sweet chilli tofu bento bowl

SERVES 4

1 tbsp sunflower oil

280g (9oz) block of extra-firm tofu, drained and pressed (see page 21)

2 tbsp sweet chilli sauce (ensure vegan)

200g (1 cup) basmati rice

2 large carrots, peeled

8cm (3in) piece of cucumber, sliced lengthways into sticks

handful of fresh edamame beans

toasted sesame seeds, for sprinkling

pinch of sea salt

The ultimate balanced lunch, which is easy to transport in a lunchbox. Use this as a basic recipe, then get creative with toasted seeds, kimchi and fresh, leafy herbs. For extra tang, serve with cheat's pink pickled onions (page 279). Delicious hot, or chilled.

1 Heat the oil in a wok over a high heat while you chop the drained and pressed tofu into bite-sized cubes. Throw in the tofu and stir-fry for 8–10 minutes until golden. Spoon in the sweet chilli sauce and stir to glaze the tofu. Remove from the heat.

2 Meanwhile, add the basmati rice to a pan and cover with cold water. Bring to the boil over a medium-high heat, then simmer for 8–10 minutes until the water has been absorbed. Remove from the heat and place a lid over the pan for 5 minutes. Use a fork to separate the rice, then season with a pinch of sea salt.

3 Use a vegetable peeler to make carrot ribbons, then place them in bowls along with the cucumber sticks and edamame beans.

4 Spoon in the sweet chilli tofu and basmati rice, then sprinkle with toasted sesame seeds. Serve hot or chilled.

EASY TIP

For the easiest way to drain and press extra-firm tofu, check out my instructions on page 21.

Eastern spiced lentils with flatbreads

SERVES 2 GENEROUSLY

Suitable for freezing

1 tbsp sunflower oil

1 onion, thinly sliced

1 tsp soft light brown sugar

½ tsp ground cumin

½ tsp ground cinnamon

1 tsp rose harissa paste

1 x 400g (14oz) can of chopped tomatoes

1 x 400g (14oz) can of green lentils, drained and rinsed

generous handful of flat-leaf parsley, roughly torn

1 tbsp shelled pistachios, roughly chopped

2 warmed flatbreads (ensure dairy-free)

generous pinch each of sea salt and black pepper

These gently spiced lentils are cooked in caramelized onions, brown sugar and harissa paste, before being scattered with fragrant flat-leaf parsley and pistachios. This is a bowl of food just made for dipping! Perfect to batch cook for comforting lunches throughout the colder months.

1 Heat the oil in a large pan, add the onion and cook over a medium heat for 5 minutes, stirring often, then scatter in the brown sugar and cook for a further 3–4 minutes until caramelized.

2 Stir in the cumin, cinnamon and harissa paste, then pour in the chopped tomatoes and green lentils. Simmer for 20 minutes, stirring occasionally.

3 Remove from the heat and stir through the flat-leaf parsley. Season to taste with sea salt and black pepper. Spoon into bowls, then scatter over the pistachios. Serve hot with warmed flatbreads.

EASY TIP

Commercially bought flatbreads can sometimes contain milk, so always check the label before purchasing. Many supermarket varieties contain oil instead of dairy products.

Microwave red lentil pâté

SERVES 4

Suitable for freezing

150g (¾ cup) dried red lentils

500ml (2 cups) hot vegetable stock

1 tbsp unsweetened soya yogurt

small handful of fresh dill, finely chopped

generous pinch each of sea salt and black pepper

drizzle of good-quality extra virgin olive oil, to serve

Nothing beats a hearty lentil pâté, served warm or chilled on toast. Being the ever-impatient lunch lover, I created this speedy microwave version, for those times when only a generous helping of pâté will do. Serve on toast triangles, crackers or crispbreads.

1 Add the lentils and vegetable stock to a large microwave-proof bowl. Cook on high for 15–17 minutes until the lentils have broken down.

2 Carefully remove from the microwave and give it a firm stir. Spoon in the soya yogurt and dill, then season to taste with sea salt and black pepper. Drizzle with a little extra virgin olive oil just before serving.

EASY TIP

This pâté will keep well when in a sealed container in the fridge for up to 3 days.

Winter tabbouleh

SERVES 2

150g (¾ cup) bulgar wheat

1 pomegranate

large handful (at least 30g/1oz)
of flat-leaf parsley, including
stems, finely chopped

juice of ½ unwaxed orange

generous drizzle of good-
quality extra virgin olive oil

small handful of walnuts,
chopped

generous pinch each of sea salt
and black pepper

I love a bowl of zesty, herby tabbouleh (eaten al fresco, of course) during the summer months. This version uses seasonal orange, walnuts and pomegranate for a fruity, jewelled version that is delicious for lunch, or as a sharing platter.

1 Add the bulgar wheat to a bowl, then pour over enough boiling water to just cover it. Place a plate or cling film (plastic wrap) over the bowl, and allow it to absorb for 15 minutes.

2 Meanwhile, slice the pomegranate in half and remove the fruity seeds, discarding the skin and any white pith.

3 Fork through the cooked bulgar wheat then add the pomegranate seeds and chopped parsley. Drizzle over the orange juice and olive oil, then season to taste with plenty of sea salt and black pepper. Mix throroughly.

4 Transfer the tabbouleh to a serving dish and scatter with walnuts. Serve warm or chilled.

EASY TIP

If you want to enjoy pomegranate without the fuss, buy pre-prepared pomegranate seeds from the supermarket.

Harissa butterbean houmous

MAKES 1 BOWLFUL

---

*Suitable for freezing
(before adding the oil)*

1 x 400g (14oz) can of
butterbeans, drained and
rinsed

2 garlic cloves, peeled

2 tbsp good-quality tahini

1 tsp rose harissa paste

juice of 1 unwaxed lemon

generous drizzle of good-
quality extra virgin olive oil

pinch of smoked sea salt

small handful of coriander
(cilantro) leaves, chopped,
to serve

1 tbsp flaked (slivered) almonds,
to serve

Step aside, chickpeas! This creamy, Moroccan-style houmous uses butterbeans for a rich, high-protein dip that is versatile enough to use in many ways. Spread onto flatbreads, use as a dip for crudités or dollop on top of salads.

1 Add the butterbeans, garlic, tahini, harissa and lemon juice to a high-powered jug blender and blitz until smooth. Add a generous drizzle of olive oil and blitz again to distribute. Season to taste with smoked sea salt.

2 Spoon out into a bowl and scatter with coriander and flaked almonds.

EASY TIP

A high-powered jug blender will blitz these ingredients into a creamy houmous; however, if you are using a stick blender, simply soak the butterbeans for 10 minutes in just-boiled water before using.

Herby yogurt and Mediterranean vegetable stuffed pittas

SERVES 2

2 rounded tbsp unsweetened soya yogurt

handful of flat-leaf parsley, finely chopped

small handful of mint leaves, finely chopped

small handful of basil leaves, finely chopped

6 cherry tomatoes, halved

6 pitted black olives, halved

2 baby sweet (bell) peppers, deseeded and sliced

2 large white pitta breads

generous pinch of black pepper

For a quick and satisfying lunch, look no further than a hot, toasted pitta bread filled with a cool, herby yogurt and fresh Mediterranean vegetables. I love white pitta for a deliciously simple flavour; seeded and wholemeal versions offer a nuttier flavour.

1 In a large bowl, stir together the yogurt, parsley, mint and basil. Then mix in the tomatoes, olives and peppers. Season to taste with black pepper.

2 Toast the pitta breads until golden, then allow to cool for 1 minute. Cut open each pitta bread to make a pocket, then load in the herby filling. Serve immediately.

EASY TIP
The herby filling can be made up to 2 days in advance when kept in a sealed container in the fridge.

Orzo minestrone

SERVES 4

Suitable for freezing

1 tbsp sunflower oil

1 onion, diced

1 celery stick, finely diced

1 carrot, peeled and thinly sliced into half-rounds

1 tsp dried mixed herbs

1 x 400g (14oz) can of chopped tomatoes

500ml (2 cups) hot vegetable stock

4 tbsp dried orzo pasta (ensure egg-free)

handful of frozen peas

small handful of basil leaves, roughly torn

generous pinch each of sea salt and black pepper

Rice-shaped orzo pasta works so well in classic minestrone soup, as its uniform shape cooks evenly and quickly, and it fits perfectly onto your spoon! Serve with warm crusty bread, for a hearty lunch.

1 Heat the oil in a large pan, add the onion, celery and carrot and cook over a medium-high heat for 3-4 minutes until the onion begins to soften but not brown. Add the dried mixed herbs and cook for 1 further minute.

2 Pour in the chopped tomatoes, vegetable stock and orzo, then simmer for 15 minutes, stirring frequently to avoid sticking.

3 Stir in the peas and cook for a further minute. Remove from the heat and season to taste with plenty of salt and pepper. Scatter with basil leaves just before serving.

EASY TIP

Stir in watercress, shredded kale or cavolo nero for extra green goodness that you can switch with the seasons.

Creamy tomato soup

SERReS 4

Suitable for freezing

1 tbsp sunflower oil

1 small onion, diced

1 x 400g (14oz) can of good-quality chopped tomatoes

500ml (2 cups) hot vegetable stock

pinch of granulated sugar

about 4 tbsp soya single (light) cream

generous pinch each of sea salt and black pepper

When I first became vegan back in 2006, I really missed creamy tomato soup. Not the fresh, chunky type, but the canned one, packaged with the famous red label. I created this simple version that uses just five ingredients, for when you just need that familiar, comforting bowl of soup.

1 In a large pan, heat the oil and onion over a medium-high heat for 2–3 minutes until softened but not browned.

2 Add the chopped tomatoes, vegetable stock and sugar, then simmer for 15 minutes.

3 Pour into a high-powered jug blender and blitz on high until completely smooth, or use a stick blender.

4 Season to taste with salt and pepper, then ladle into bowls. Swirl through the soya cream, about a tablespoon per bowl.

EASY TIP

Blitzing the soup in a high-powered jug blender will make it extra creamy. If you don't have a high-powered blender, use a stick blender but blitz for a little longer to ensure it is smooth.

Sundried tomato and oregano scones

MAKES 8

Suitable for freezing

250g (2 cups) plain (all-purpose) flour, plus extra for rolling

1 tsp bicarbonate of soda (baking soda)

1 tsp dried oregano

5 sundried tomatoes in oil, roughly chopped

120ml (½ cup) unsweetened soya milk, plus extra for glazing

generous pinch each of sea salt and black pepper

These perfectly portable scones are a tasty alternative to a sandwich, especially when served at a picnic. Delicious served warm, with lashings of cool vegan cream cheese.

1 Preheat the oven to 220°C/425°F/gas mark 7 and line a baking sheet with baking parchment.

2 In a large bowl, mix together the flour, bicarbonate of soda, dried oregano, and some sea salt and black pepper.

3 Stir through the chopped sundried tomatoes until coated in the flour mix, then stir in the soya milk and combine into a thick dough.

4 Place the dough on a lightly floured surface, then roll to a 2cm (¾in) thickness. Use a scone cutter to cut out the scones, then place them on the lined baking tray. Brush the tops with a little soya milk, then bake in the oven for 10–12 minutes until lightly golden.

EASY TIP
Switch up the recipe by adding sliced black olives, capers and fresh chopped herbs.

MINUTE.
15
MINUTE.

Antipasti platter

SERVES 2

1 small baguette (French stick), sliced

generous drizzle of good-quality extra virgin olive oil

handful of mixed olives

4 sundried tomatoes, drained of excess oil

4 chargrilled peppers in oil, drained of excess oil

handful of shelled walnuts

8 cherry tomatoes, halved

a few basil leaves

pinch of black pepper

Sometimes, you just need to graze on some chargrilled, sundried and marinated vegetables, with warm bread and excellent olive oil. A simple but indulgent lunch, which doubles as an impressive starter to serve to guests before dinner.

1 Place a griddle (grill) pan over a high heat, then lay on the baguette slices and toast for 1–2 minutes on each side until golden. Remove from the heat and drizzle with extra virgin olive oil.

2 In the meantime, arrange the olives, sundried tomatoes, chargrilled peppers and walnuts in small piles on a serving plate or board. Season the cherry tomatoes with black pepper and place them on the board, then scatter over a few basil leaves.

3 Serve the antipasti platter with the warm, toasted bread.

EASY TIP

Jars of antipasti vegetables including olives, sundried tomatoes and chargrilled peppers keep well in the fridge, and can be used to prepare a quick lunch, or stirred through pasta for an easy supper.

Warm panzanella

SERVES 2 GENEROUSLY

300g (10oz) cherry tomatoes (or use larger ones, quartered or halved)

½ small red onion, thinly sliced

4 chargrilled peppers in oil, drained of excess oil

2 thick slices of white bread, torn into bite-sized chunks

drizzle of good-quality extra virgin olive oil

small handful of flat-leaf parsley, finely chopped

gernerous pinch each of sea salt and black pepper

I love panzanella – the rustic bread and tomato salad – but often find the mix of raw tomatoes and red onion a little acidic. By gently oven-baking the ingredients, the flavours are softened. Go liberal with the extra virgin olive oil, for a hit of fruitiness over the mellow flavours.

1 Preheat the oven to 200°C/400°F/gas mark 6.

2 Arrange the tomatoes, red onion, peppers and bread in an ovenproof dish, then bake in the oven for 15 minutes.

3 Remove from the oven and drizzle with extra virgin olive oil. Season with salt and pepper, toss, then scatter with parsley.

EASY TIP

Revive bread slices that are almost destined for the bin in this warming salad.

Seville salad

SERVES 2 GENEROUSLY

½ small red onion, thinly sliced

2 unwaxed oranges, peeled and sliced into rounds

1 large beef tomato, thinly sliced

handful of black or kalamata olives, pitted

small handful of flat-leaf parsley, finely chopped

generous pinch each of sea salt and black pepper

Reminisce about warm Spanish holidays with this simple yet flavoursome salad. I don't find that this salad needs any extra virgin olive oil (the black olives and orange slices deliver on moisture) but feel free to add a drizzle, if you like.

1 Add the onion slices to a bowl and cover with boiling water. Allow to stand for 15 minutes until the onions soften slightly, then drain away the liquid.

2 Arrange the soaked red onion, sliced orange, sliced tomato and olives on a serving plate, then scatter with flat-leaf parsley. Season with a pinch of salt and pepper.

EASY TIP

Allowing the red onion slices to stand in hot water for 15 minutes takes away the initial acidity and sharpness, and helps them to soften a little.

Mexican sweetcorn and avocado salad

SERVES 2

165g (1 cup) drained and rinsed canned sweetcorn

1 red (bell) pepper, deseeded and finely diced

2 spring onions (scallions), finely chopped

handful of cherry tomatoes, quartered

small handful of coriander (cilantro) leaves, roughly torn

juice of ½ unwaxed lime

generous handful of wild rocket (arugula)

1 avocado, peeled, stoned and sliced

generous pinch each of smoked sea salt and black pepper

This quick salad recipe is handy for lunchtimes when you don't have the time to prepare something extravagant, but need something full of flavour, with a satisfying crunch. Peppery wild rocket is topped with lime-dressed sweetcorn salad, finished with cool avocado. I love to season this salad with a little smoked sea salt for an extra layer of flavour, but if you don't have this available, good-quality sea salt flakes will do the trick.

1 In a large bowl, stir together the sweetcorn, diced pepper, spring onions, cherry tomatoes and coriander. Squeeze through the lime juice.

2 Arrange the wild rocket on two plates (or one large serving plate) and spoon over the sweetcorn mix. Lay over the avocado slices, then season with smoked sea salt and black pepper.

EASY TIP

If you don't have a can of sweetcorn available, frozen sweetcorn makes an excellent alternative. Simply cook in a pan of simmering water for 3–4 minutes, then rinse in cool water before using.

Guacamole tortilla pinwheels

SERVES 2

1 ripe avocado, halved

4 cherry tomatoes, finely chopped

2 spring onions (scallions), finely chopped

juice of ½ unwaxed lime

2 large white tortilla wraps

generous pinch of sea salt

These fun, bite-sized wraps are loved by grown-ups and kids alike, making them the perfect addition to lunchboxes, no matter your age. I love to shake a few drops of Tabasco into the guacamole, but I'll let you decide if you prefer to add the heat!

1 Scoop the flesh from the avocado into a large bowl, use a fork to mash the avocado roughly, then stir in the cherry tomatoes, spring onions, lime juice and sea salt.

2 Lay out the wraps on a flat surface, then evenly spread over the guacamole over the surface of each wrap, to the edges.

3 Starting at one end, tightly roll the wrap inwards to form a log shape. Use a sharp knife to cut the roll into 6 even pinwheels.

EASY TIP

Prepare the guacamole up to a day in advance – the addition of fresh lime juice will help to prevent the avocado from browning. Simply keep in the fridge in a sealed container.

Cheat's spiced baked beans

SERVES 2

1 tbsp sunflower oil

1 onion, thinly sliced

1 garlic clove, crushed

½ tsp ground cumin

½ tsp ground turmeric

pinch of dried chilli flakes

1 x 400g (14oz) can of baked beans in tomato sauce

small handful of coriander (cilantro), finely chopped

generous pinch each of smoked sea salt and black pepper

The humble can of baked beans is a British store cupboard classic, but the addition of a few extra ingredients can transform baked beans into a whole new dish. Caramelized onions, garlic and spices deliver on maximum flavour, while chopped coriander freshens everything up. Serve over baked potatoes or toast, or in a dish with a warm vegan naan bread.

1 Heat the oil in a medium pan, add the onion and soften over a low-medium heat for 8–10 minutes until it begins to turn golden-brown. Add the garlic, cumin, turmeric and chilli flakes and cook for a further 1–2 minutes, stirring frequently to avoid sticking.

2 Pour in the baked beans (including the tomato sauce from the can) and continue to stir for 2–3 minutes until the beans are heated through, and the onion and spices are combined.

3 Remove from the heat and stir in the coriander. Season to taste with salt and pepper. Serve hot.

EASY TIP

Add more or fewer chilli flakes, depending on how spicy you want the baked beans to be. Remember that heat from chillies will increase with each mouthful, so keep some coconut yogurt close by to stir through!

Pizza nacho stack

SERVES 2 GENEROUSLY

2 large white tortilla wraps, sliced into small nacho-sized triangles

drizzle of sunflower oil

generous pinch of dried chilli flakes

pinch of dried oregano

8 cherry tomatoes, quartered

½ small red onion, thinly sliced

handful of grated vegan hard cheese

small handful of pitted black olives, sliced into rounds

small handful of basil leaves

generous pinch each of sea salt and black pepper

How do you make nachos even better? Throw in all the flavours of pizza! This is a generous sized portion for two people, for a casual lunch, or snack at any time.

1 Preheat the oven to 180°C/350°F/gas mark 4.

2 Arrange the tortilla triangles over 2 baking trays and rub over the sunflower oil. Sprinkle with the chilli flakes, oregano and salt and pepper.

3 Add the cherry tomatoes and red onion slices to the baking trays, dotted around the tortilla triangles, then bake in the oven for 8 minutes until the tortillas have begun to turn golden. Carefully remove from the oven and scatter with grated vegan cheese. Return to the oven for a further 2 minutes.

4 Remove the trays from the oven and arrange on a serving plate. Scatter with olives and basil leaves just before serving.

EASY TIP

This is a great way to use up those tortilla wraps that would otherwise end up in the bin! Tortilla wraps also freeze well without affecting the texture, and defrost in minutes.

Cajun bean, avocado and coriander wraps

SERVES 4

*Suitable for freezing
(filling only)*

1 tbsp sunflower oil

1 red onion, sliced

1 x 400g (14oz) can of red
kidney beans, drained and
thoroughly rinsed

1 tsp Cajun seasoning

juice of ½ unwaxed lime

4 large white tortilla wraps

1 avocado, peeled, stoned
and sliced

handful of baby spinach leaves,
tough stalks removed

small handful of coriander
(cilantro) leaves

4 tbsp vegan mayonnaise

**Some lunchbreaks are just calling out for a soft tortilla
wrap loaded with spiced beans, red onion and creamy
avocado. Freeze the cooked bean mixture in single-serve
portions, then defrost and reheat as needed, with plenty
of coriander, spinach and vegan mayonnaise.**

1 Heat the oil in a wok, add the red onion and cook for
3–4 minutes until softened. Add the kidney beans and
Cajun seasoning and stir-fry for 2–3 minutes until the onion
and the beans are coated in the seasoning. Remove from
the heat and squeeze over the lime juice.

2 Lay out the wraps and arrange a few slices of avocado
on each. Spoon in the spicy beans then add the spinach
and coriander and top with a tablespoon of vegan
mayonnaise in each wrap. Fold the sides of each wrap
inwards, then roll up to envelop the filling.

EASY TIP
Switch red kidney beans for canned black beans or
cannellini beans, depending on what you have available
in your cupboard.

Crushed white bean and dill smørrebrød with quick-pickled radish

SERVES 2 GENEROUSLY

2 radishes, thinly sliced

2 tbsp apple cider vinegar

1 x 400g (14oz) can of cannellini beans, drained and rinsed

1 tbsp vegan cream cheese

handful of fresh dill, finely chopped

drizzle of good-quality extra virgin olive oil

4 slices of rye bread

generous pinch each of sea salt and black pepper

A smørrebrød is a delicious open sandwich, with a topping served over nutty rye bread. This speedy version uses cannellini beans, vegan cream cheese and dill for a luxurious topping, while quick-pickled radishes bring some zing and a little heat.

1 Add the sliced radishes to a small bowl and pour over the cider vinegar. Allow to infuse while you prepare the rest of the sandwich.

2 Add the cannellini beans to a bowl and use a fork to roughly break up the beans. Stir in the cream cheese, dill and a drizzle of extra virgin olive oil and mix to combine. Season to taste with salt and pepper.

3 Lightly toast the rye bread, then spoon the bean mix over each slice. Top with the quick-pickled radishes, then serve while the toast is warm.

QUICK TIP
The bean mix will last for up to 3 days in a sealed container in the fridge. It can also be used to load onto bagels and over baked potatoes.

Ultimate ALT

SERVES 2

2 tbsp barbecue sauce
(ensure vegan)

2 tsp tomato ketchup

1 tsp sunflower oil

½ tsp smoked paprika

1 small aubergine (eggplant),
cut into long slices, about 3mm
(⅛in) thick

4 thick slices of sourdough
bread

1 tsp vegan butter

2 iceberg lettuce leaves

1 beef tomato, evenly sliced

generous pinch of smoked sea
salt

**ALT is the new BLT. Smoky aubergine is baked until
crispy at the edges, before being sandwiched in thick,
toasted sourdough, with slices of beef tomato and
lettuce. A sandwich doesn't get more ultimate than this.**

1 Preheat the oven to 180°C/350°F/gas mark 4 and line
a baking tray with baking parchment.

2 In a small bowl, whisk together the barbecue sauce,
ketchup, sunflower oil and smoked paprika. Use a pastry
brush to coat both sides of the aubergine slices in the
barbecue sauce mix, then place on the lined baking tray.
Sprinkle with smoked sea salt. Bake in the oven for
40–45 minutes until the aubergine has softened in the
centre and become crisp at the edges.

3 In the meantime, toast the bread slices until lightly
golden and spread one side with vegan butter.

4 Place the lettuce on the base slice of the sandwich,
followed by a couple of slices of beef tomato.

5 Remove the sliced aubergine from the oven. Use tongs
to generously place slices over the tomato, then complete
the sandwich with the remaining slice of bread. Cut with
a sharp knife and serve while the aubergine is hot.

EASY TIP

Use a sharp knife or mandoline to slice the aubergine into
thin slices – the thinner the slices, the crisper the smoked
aubergine 'rashers' will be!

Cheesy roasted broccoli soup

SERVES 4

Suitable for freezing

1 medium head of broccoli, broken into florets and tough stems removed

1 tbsp sunflower oil

4 tbsp vegan cream cheese

500ml (2 cups) hot vegetable stock

200ml (generous ¾ cup) unsweetened soya milk

pinch of grated nutmeg

handful of chives, finely chopped

generous pinch each of sea salt and black pepper

Hug in a bowl, anyone? Combine humble broccoli with vegan cream cheese for a silky, smooth, slurpy soup that everyone will love. Serve with crusty bread and lashings of vegan butter.

1 Preheat the oven to 180°C/350°F/gas mark 4.

2 Arrange the broccoli florets on a baking tray and drizzle with sunflower oil. Roast in the oven for 15–20 minutes until softened.

3 Remove the roasted broccoli from the oven, then spoon into a high-powered jug blender. Add the vegan cream cheese, vegetable stock and soya milk then blitz on high until completely smooth.

4 Stir through the grated nutmeg and chives. Season to taste with salt and pepper.

EASY TIP

Vegan cream cheese can be found in large supermarkets. The base ingredient varies from brand to brand, but is often made from coconut, soya or almond, with or without additional flavours, including herbs and garlic. Choose a plain version for this recipe.

Supper

POT · POT
1
POT · POT

Herby roasted grapes with squash and lentils

SERVES 2

Suitable for freezing

1 x 400g (14oz) can of green lentils, drained and rinsed

1 tsp dried sage

2 tbsp sunflower oil

150g (3 cups) red grapes

1 small butternut squash, peeled and thinly sliced into half-rounds

1 sprig of fresh rosemary

generous pinch each of sea salt and black pepper

I love to cook this simple supper on a cold, autumn evening then eat it from a bowl. Cosy, comforting and perfectly balanced, this dish will become your new midweek staple. Serve alone or with fail-safe roast potatoes (page 291).

1 Preheat the oven to 180°C/350°F/gas mark 4.

2 In a large bowl, stir together the lentils, sage, 1 tablespoon of the sunflower oil and grapes.

3 Spoon the mixture into a large, deep roasting tray. Lay the butternut squash slices evenly in the tray and drizzle with the remaining tablespoon of sunflower oil. Place the sprig of rosemary in the centre of the tray, then loosely cover the tray with foil and bake in the oven for 30 minutes.

4 Carefully remove the foil from the tray and bake for a further 15–20 minutes until the squash has softened.

5 Remove the tray from the oven and discard the rosemary. Season to taste with salt and pepper. Serve hot.

EASY TIP

If you struggle to peel the tough skin on butternut squash, simply cook the squash in a microwave for up to 2 minutes to soften before peeling.

Roasted onion tart

SERVES 4

4 onions, peeled and halved

generous drizzle of sunflower oil

3 sprigs of rosemary

1 sheet of ready rolled puff pastry (ensure dairy-free)

1 tsp unsweetened soya milk, for brushing

small handful of flat-leaf parsley, finely chopped

generous pinch each of sea salt and black pepper

Let the oven do all of the hard work by transforming simple onions into a sweet, caramelized topping for vegan puff pastry. Many brands of puff pastry available in supermarkets use vegetable fat instead of butter, making them accidentally vegan, but always check the ingredients list before you buy. Simple, hearty and satisfying.

1 Preheat the oven to 180°C/350°F/gas mark 4.

2 Arrange the onions face up in a roasting tin and drizzle with sunflower oil. Lay the sprigs of rosemary in the tin, then roast in the oven for 30 minutes.

3 Increase the temperature of the oven to 200°C/400°F/gas mark 5 and roast for a further 25 minutes until golden and caramelized.

4 Meanwhile, line a baking tray with baking parchment and lay out the puff pastry sheet. Fold in the edges by approximately 2cm (¾ in) and brush with a little soya milk. Pierce the centre of the pastry with a fork (to allow the steam to release during cooking and prevent the centre rising). Bake in the oven for 10–12 minutes until golden.

5 Remove the roasted onions and cooked pastry from the oven. Spoon the onion halves onto the pastry, dishevelling them a little as you do, for a rustic appearance. Scatter with a little flat-leaf parsley, then season to taste with sea salt and black pepper.

EASY TIP

Roasting the onions in a separate baking dish to the pastry, then assembling just before serving, creates the perfect supper, without a soggy bottom on the pastry!

Italian barley stew with white beans and greens

SERVES 4

Suitable for freezing

1 tbsp sunflower oil

1 onion, diced

1 large carrot, peeled and chopped into half-rounds

1 celery stick, diced

2 garlic cloves, crushed

1 tsp dried oregano

1 x 400g (14oz) can of good-quality chopped tomatoes

600ml (2½ cups) hot vegetable stock

4 tbsp pearl barley

1 dried bay leaf

1 x 400g (14oz) can of cannellini beans, drained and rinsed

4 stalks of cavolo nero, roughly sliced, tough stems discarded

generous pinch each of sea salt and black pepper

This supper is simple, hearty comfort food, that is best eaten from a bowl with a spoon. Serve with wedges of warm, crusty bread.

1 Heat the oil in a large pan over a medium-high heat. Throw in the onion, carrot and celery and cook for 2–3 minutes until the onion begins to soften. Stir in the garlic and oregano, then cook for a further 2 minutes.

2 Pour in the chopped tomatoes and vegetable stock, then spoon in the pearl barley. Add the bay leaf and reduce the heat to medium, then cook for 25 minutes, stirring frequently.

3 Discard the bay leaf before stirring in the cannellini beans and cavolo nero. Cook for a further 5–6 minutes.

4 Remove from the heat and season to taste with sea salt and plenty of black pepper.

EASY TIP

If you prefer a thicker stew, add another tablespoon of pearl barley and reduce down for a further 10 minutes, stirring often.

INGREDIENTS · 5

Tagliatelle alla norma

SERVES 2 GENEROUSLY

1 aubergine (eggplant), sliced into 4cm (1½in) wedges

2 tbsp sunflower oil

200g (7oz) dried tagliatelle (ensure egg-free)

2 garlic cloves, crushed

300g (10oz) good-quality passata (sieved tomatoes)

handful of flat-leaf parsley, finely chopped

generous pinch each of sea salt and black pepper

This summery, Sicilian-inspired dish is a real go-to for a satisfying supper. Traditionally, aubergines are fried for this dish, however I love to roast them in the oven for a tender texture and slightly smoked flavour. Many brands of dried pasta are egg-free (but always check the ingredients), so choose your favourite; I love to use tagliatelle for a slippery, satisfying bowl of pasta.

1 Preheat the oven to 220°C/425°F/gas mark 7.

2 Arrange the sliced aubergine on a baking tray and drizzle with half the sunflower oil. Roast in the oven for 20 minutes until softened.

3 Meanwhile, bring a large pan of salted water to the boil. Add the tagliatelle and cook for 8–10 minutes until *al dente*, then thoroughly drain.

4 While the pasta is cooking, add the remaining tablespoon of oil to another pan and cook the garlic over a medium heat for 2 minutes. Pour in the passata and simmer for 5 minutes, stirring frequently. Remove from the heat and season to taste with sea salt and plenty of black pepper.

5 Remove the aubergine from the oven and stir into the sauce. Use tongs to toss the pasta into the sauce and stir through the parsley, then serve.

EASY TIP

Choose a good-quality passata for a perfectly sweet flavour, or add in a pinch of sugar with the passata to balance the acidity.

MINUTE. MINUTE. 15

Vodka cream gnocchi

SERVES 2

The sauce is suitable for freezing

1 tbsp sunflower oil

1 garlic clove, crushed

500g (2 cups/17oz) good-quality passata (sieved tomatoes)

pinch of sugar

4 tbsp soya single (light) cream

100ml (scant ½ cup) vodka

500g (1lb 2oz) potato gnocchi (ensure egg-free)

handful of small basil leaves

generous pinch each of sea salt and black pepper

This indulgent supper is as simple as it is delicious, with a vodka-infused sauce. Vodka helps to emulsify acidic tomatoes and dairy-free cream, as well as bringing out a sweeter flavour in the tomato passata. Team this sauce with gnocchi, for a comforting bowlful.

1 Add the oil and garlic to a large pan and cook over a medium heat for 1 minute until the oil is infused. Pour in the passata and sugar and cook for 2–3 minutes.

2 Spoon in the soya cream and vodka and lay a lid loosely over the pan. Simmer for 10 minutes, stirring occasionally.

3 Meanwhile, bring a separate pan of salted water to the boil and add the gnocchi. Cook for 2–3 minutes until *al dente*, then thoroughly drain away the water.

4 Season the sauce to taste with salt and plenty of pepper, then remove from the heat. Add the cooked gnocchi and stir to coat in the sauce. Scatter over the basil leaves just before serving.

EASY TIP
Prepared potato gnocchi can be found in most supermarkets, many of which don't contain egg, but always check the label before purchasing. It's useful to keep in the cupboard for a quick supper as it cooks in minutes.

MINUTE. MINUTE. 15

Kale pesto pasta

SERVES 2

160g (1½ cups) dried farfalle
pasta (ensure egg-free)

4 generous handfuls of kale,
finely shredded (tough stems
discarded)

2 tbsp olive oil

1 garlic clove, crushed

pinch of dried chilli flakes

small handful of pine nuts

handful of flat-leaf parsley,
finely chopped

zest and juice of ½ unwaxed
lemon

generous pinch each of sea salt
and black pepper

**For those evenings where you need a fast dinner, that
is also ready in just one pot, welcome this pesto pasta
with a twist. Kale and flat-leaf parsley replace traditional
basil for a nutritious bowl of comfort food. I love to use
butterfly-shaped farfalle pasta to hold the delicious
pesto, but feel free to use your favourite egg-free pasta,
or what you have available in your store cupboard.**

1 Bring a large pan of salted water to the boil, then add
the pasta and kale. Simmer for 8–10 minutes until the
pasta is *al dente*, then drain. Leave the cooked pasta and
kale in the colander and return the pan to the hob.

2 Heat the oil, garlic, chilli flakes and pine nuts in the
pan over a medium heat for 2 minutes until the garlic
is fragrant and softened.

3 Toss in the pasta and kale, along with the chopped
parsley, and stir through. Remove from the heat and
stir in the lemon zest and juice. Season to taste with
salt and pepper.

EASY TIP
Use a fine colander or sieve to drain the water away from
the pan, to ensure that the finely shredded kale doesn't
end up in the sink!

Simple aubergine parmigiana

SERVES 4

Suitable for freezing

1 tbsp sunflower oil, plus extra for brushing

2 large aubergines (eggplants), sliced lengthways into 5mm (¼in) slices

3 garlic cloves, crushed

2 tsp dried oregano

2 x 400g (14oz) cans of chopped tomatoes

150g (5oz) vegan mozzarella cheese, thinly sliced

generous pinch each of sea salt and black pepper

Simple, light and fragrant, this aubergine parmigiana makes the perfect midweek meal that everyone will love. Serve with a crisp, green salad and a rustic baguette.

1 Preheat the oven to 200°C/400°F/gas mark 6.

2 Brush sunflower oil onto the aubergine slices and place in a large frying pan. Cook over a high heat for 2–3 minutes on each side, then remove from the heat and allow to stand for a few minutes.

3 In the meantime, soften the garlic in the tablespoon of sunflower oil over a medium heat, then add the oregano and chopped tomatoes. Cook for 10 minutes, stirring occasionally.

4 Arrange slices of aubergine in a deep baking dish, followed by a layer of the tomato sauce and slices of the vegan mozzarella. Repeat until the dish is full, finishing with a layer of tomato sauce.

5 Bake in the oven for 25–30 minutes, then serve hot.

EASY TIP

Vegan mozzarella can be found in most supermarkets, simply look in the free-from section. Vegan cheddar works well as an alternative too.

Creamy basil baked shells

SERVES 4

16 dried giant pasta shells (ensure egg-free)

1 tbsp sunflower oil

3 garlic cloves, crushed

2 x 400g (14oz) cans of good-quality chopped tomatoes

200g (1 cup) vegan cream cheese

large handful of basil, very finely chopped (leave a few small leaves whole for topping)

generous pinch each of sea salt and black pepper

Comforting and creamy, these pasta shells (giant conchiglioni) are stuffed with vegan cream cheese and basil, before being baked in a fragrant tomato sauce. Serve with garlic bread and a fresh rocket salad.

1 Preheat the oven to 180°C/350°F/gas mark 4.

2 Bring a large pan of salted water to the boil, then add the pasta shells. Cook for 8 minutes until *al dente* (they will finish cooking in the oven), then drain. Rinse with cold water until they are cool enough to handle.

3 Meanwhile, heat the oil and garlic over a low-medium heat in a separate pan for 2 minutes until fragrant and softened. Stir in the chopped tomatoes and simmer for 5 minutes. Season to taste with sea salt and plenty of black pepper. Pour into a large, deep ovenproof dish and set aside.

4 In a bowl, stir together the vegan cream cheese and the chopped basil. Spoon the cream cheese into the pasta shells then place them over the tomato sauce in the ovenproof dish.

5 Loosely cover with foil, then bake in the oven for 25–30 minutes. Remove from the oven and scatter with the reserved basil leaves just before serving.

EASY TIP
The tomato and garlic base sauce can be made up to 3 days in advance, or frozen and defrosted before use for a speedier dish.

POT · POT ·
1
· POT · POT

Summer ratatouille

SERVES 4

Suitable for freezing

1 tbsp sunflower oil

1 onion, roughly chopped

1 aubergine (eggplant), roughly diced

2 courgettes (zucchini), roughly diced

1 yellow (bell) pepper, deseeded and roughly chopped

150g (1 cup) cherry tomatoes

1 tsp dried oregano

1 tsp dried mixed herbs

1 x 400g (14oz) can of good-quality chopped tomatoes

2 tbsp pitted green olives

small handful of small basil leaves

generous pinch each of sea salt and black pepper

This is my favourite ratatouille recipe and is a regular in my kitchen during the summer months, when I want something comforting but still fresh. Controversially, I love to throw in a few olives for seasoning and pops of flavour. It elevates the flavour, with minimal effort on your behalf. Serve with slices of crusty bread, and a glass of cold cider, al fresco of course.

1 Heat the oil in a large pan, add the onion, aubergine and courgette and cook over a medium-high heat for 4–5 minutes, stirring frequently. Throw in the yellow pepper, tomatoes, oregano and mixed herbs, then cook for a further 2 minutes.

2 Pour in the chopped tomatoes and olives, then simmer over a medium heat for 25 minutes, stirring occasionally.

3 Remove from the heat and season to taste with sea salt and plenty of black pepper. Scatter over the basil leaves just before serving.

EASY TIP
Save any leftovers to stir through pasta for another simple, summery supper.

Sweetcorn, spring onion and chilli fritters

SERVES 2

100g (scant 1 cup) plain (all-purpose) flour

2 tsp baking powder

2 spring onions (scallions), finely chopped

1 small red chilli, deseeded and finely chopped

small handful of coriander (cilantro), finely chopped

200g (1¼ cups) drained and rinsed canned sweetcorn

4 tbsp sunflower oil

generous pinch of smoked sea salt

These fritters are perfect for when you have very little in the fridge, but still need something to satisfy your hunger. Reduce or leave out the red chilli if serving to younger diners, or those who just prefer milder fritters. Serve with pea and avocado guacamole (page 302) or wedges of unwaxed lime for squeezing, if you like.

1 In a bowl, mix together the flour, baking powder and smoked sea salt. Stir in the spring onions, chilli and coriander, then mix in 120ml (½ cup) cold water to create a smooth batter.

2 Stir in the sweetcorn until it is coated in the batter.

3 Heat the sunflower oil in a frying pan over a medium heat. Drop tablespoon-sized amounts of the mix into the hot oil and cook for 2–3 minutes on each side until golden and slightly risen.

EASY TIP
Frozen sweetcorn also works well in this recipe; ensure it is defrosted before using.

Giant Greek beans

SERVES 2

Suitable for freezing

1 tbsp sunflower oil

1 onion, diced

2 garlic cloves, crushed

1 tsp smoked paprika

1 tsp dried oregano

1 x 400g (14oz) can of chopped tomatoes

1 x 400g (14oz) can of butterbeans, drained and rinsed

pinch of granulated sugar

handful of pitted black olives

generous handful of fresh flat-leaf parsley, finely chopped

small handful of dill, finely chopped

generous pinch each of sea salt and black pepper

Giant Greek beans or *gigantes plaki* is a traditional Mediterranean dish, usually slow-cooked for many hours, using dried beans. This speedy, weeknight-friendly version uses canned butterbeans so you can enjoy a taste of Greece without leaving your house. Serve with warm, crusty bread.

1 Heat the oil and onion in a large pan over a medium-high heat for 2–3 minutes until the onion begins to soften. Add the garlic, paprika and oregano and cook for a further 2 minutes.

2 Pour in the chopped tomatoes, butterbeans and sugar then cook for 15–20 minutes until the sauce has started to reduce a little.

3 Remove from the heat, then stir in the olives, flat-leaf parsley and dill. Season to taste with salt and pepper.

EASY TIP

A pinch of sugar reduces the acidity of the canned tomatoes, resulting in a mellow, summery flavour.

Leek, pear and potato hash

SERVES 2 GENEROUSLY

Suitable for freezing

4 tbsp sunflower oil

2 large baking potatoes, scrubbed clean and diced into 1cm (½in) cubes

1 leek, finely chopped

10 button mushrooms, brushed clean and halved

2 conference pears, roughly sliced

small handful of sage, leaves finely chopped, plus 4 leaves reserved for garnish

generous pinch each of sea salt and black pepper

This simple supper is perfect for an autumnal midweek meal. I love serving this with a spoonful of brown sauce, and a side of baked beans. Comfort food at its best!

1 Heat half the oil in a large frying pan and cook the potatoes over a medium-high heat for 10 minutes, stirring frequently until they start to become golden.

2 Add the leek and mushrooms, then cook for a further 5 minutes, stirring frequently to avoid sticking. Stir in the pears and sage and cook for a further 2–3 minutes.

3 Heat the remaining oil in a small frying pan then add the reserved sage leaves and fry for 1–2 minutes until crisp. Leave to drain on some kitchen paper (they will crisp up more as they cool).

4 Season the hash to taste with salt and pepper, then serve hot topped with the fried sage leaves.

EASY TIP
Switch up the flavour by swapping the sage for rosemary or thyme.

Spanish chickpea and olive stew

SERVES 4

Suitable for freezing

1 tbsp sunflower oil

1 onion, diced

1 yellow (bell) pepper, deseeded and thinly sliced

1 garlic clove, crushed

1 tsp smoked paprika

1 tsp dried thyme

1 x 400g (14oz) can of chopped tomatoes

1 x 400g (14oz) can of chickpeas (garbanzo beans), drained and rinsed

handful of pitted black olives

generous handful of flat-leaf parsley, finely chopped

2 rounded tbsp flaked (slivered) almonds

generous pinch each of sea salt and black pepper

Simple suppers are the best kind of supper. Chickpeas, olives and peppers are simmered in a smoky, herby sauce, topped with crunchy toasted almonds. Toasting the almonds in a dry pan takes just a couple of minutes, but it's well worth it for the extra layer of flavour it brings. Serve with paprika potato rounds (page 280).

1 Heat the oil in a large pan or heatproof casserole dish, add the onion and pepper and cook over a medium-high heat for 3–4 minutes until they begin to soften. Add the garlic, smoked paprika and thyme and cook for a further minute.

2 Pour in the chopped tomatoes and chickpeas, then simmer over a medium heat for 20 minutes, stirring occasionally.

3 Stir in the olives and cook for a further 2 minutes, then remove from the heat. Season to taste with salt and pepper, then stir through the parsley.

4 Toast the flaked almonds in a dry frying pan until lightly golden and fragrant. Scatter over the stew just before serving.

EASY TIP
If you happen to have any leftovers, stir in some hot vegetable stock then blitz in a high-powered blender for a tasty soup.

Sausage, apple and bean casserole

SERVES 2 GENEROUSLY

Suitable for freezing

6 vegan sausages

1 tbsp sunflower oil

1 onion, finely chopped

2 carrots, peeled and finely chopped

1 celery stick, finely diced

1 tsp dried rosemary

1 tsp dried sage

generous glug of red wine (ensure vegan)

1 x 400g (14oz) can of chopped tomatoes

1 x 400g (14oz) can of cannellini beans, drained and rinsed

1 apple, roughly sliced

generous pinch each of sea salt and black pepper

For the ultimate in comfort food, make a pot of this casserole, which can be ready in 30 minutes. I love to serve this with mashed potatoes, or some crusty bread for dipping. Perfect for a cosy night in, with a glass of red wine.

1 Cook the vegan sausages using your preferred cooking method (or follow the packet instructions) while you prepare the casserole.

2 Heat the oil in a large heatproof casserole pot or pan, add the onion, carrots and celery and cook down over a medium-high heat for 5 minutes, stirring occasionally. Sprinkle in the rosemary and sage and cook for 1 further minute.

3 Pour in the wine and cook for 2–3 minutes, allowing it to reduce slightly.

4 Pour in the chopped tomatoes, cannellini beans and apple and simmer for 15 minutes until the tomatoes have reduced a little.

5 Remove from the heat and add in the cooked vegan sausages. Season to taste with salt and pepper.

EASY TIP

I find that cooking vegan sausages separately to the casserole helps them to keep their shape and texture.

Pantry root stew

SERVES 4

Suitable for freezing

1 tbsp sunflower oil

1 onion, diced

1 carrot, peeled and thinly sliced

1 celery stick, thinly sliced

1 parsnip, peeled and thinly sliced

1 tsp dried sage

glug of red wine (ensure vegan)

1 x 400g (14oz) can of chopped tomatoes

1 x 300g (10oz) can of new potatoes, drained and rinsed

1 x 400g (14oz) can of butterbeans, drained and rinsed

1 sprig of fresh rosemary

1 sprig of fresh thyme

2 bay leaves

generous pinch each of sea salt and black pepper

The terms '15-minute' and 'stew' don't normally go together, but this version uses a handful of quick-cook root vegetables, alongside canned potatoes, reducing the cooking time of this stew significantly. There's often a sense of snobbery around canned potatoes, but they are handy to have in the store cupboard: they reduce peeling and cooking time, absorb flavours well and are cost-effective.

1 Heat the oil in a large pan, add the onion, carrot, celery, parsnip and sage and cook over a high heat for 2–3 minutes, stirring constantly, until the onion begins to soften. Pour in the red wine and reduce down for 2 minutes.

2 Stir in the chopped tomatoes, then add the potatoes and butterbeans. Drop in the rosemary, thyme and bay leaves, then cook for 10 minutes, stirring frequently.

3 Remove from the heat and season to taste with salt and pepper. Discard the woody herb sprigs and bay leaves just before serving.

EASY TIP

Make this stew stretch even further by adding a 400g (14oz) can of green lentils.

Creamy squash and Puy lentil pie

SERVES 4

1 tbsp sunflower oil

½ butternut squash, peeled, deseeded and cut into 2cm (¾in) dice

1 red onion, diced

1 tsp dried sage

2 garlic cloves, crushed

1 x 400g (14oz) can of Puy lentils (or use vacuum-packed), drained and rinsed

200ml (¾ cup) soya single (light) cream

2 sheets of filo pastry (ensure dairy-free)

generous pinch each of sea salt and black pepper

This effortless pie looks rustic, tastes like autumn and takes just 30 minutes to put together – perfect for midweek suppers that all of the family will love. Many brands of pre-made filo pastry contain vegetable oil instead of butter, making it suitable for vegans, but do check the label before you buy. Serve with mashed potatoes and freshly steamed broccoli, or a green salad for a lighter option.

1 Heat the oil in a large pan, add the butternut squash and onion and cook over a medium-high heat for 8–10 minutes until the squash begins to soften. Add the sage and garlic and cook for a further 2–3 minutes.

2 Meanwhile, preheat the oven to 200°C/400°F/gas mark 6.

3 Stir the lentils into the pan, then pour in the soya cream and season with sea salt and plenty of black pepper. Stir to distribute then transfer to a deep pie dish.

4 Tear the sheets of filo pastry into strips, then arrange them over the top of the pie filling, scrunching and positioning them randomly until the top is covered.

5 Bake in the oven for 15 minutes until the filo pastry becomes golden.

EASY TIP

Frozen butternut squash also works well in this recipe, but do make sure that the chunks are softened in the pan before cooking the pie in the oven.

Pot au feu with white beans

SERVES 4

Suitable for freezing

1 tbsp sunflower oil

1 medium leek, thinly sliced

1 celery stick, finely chopped

1 carrot, peeled and thinly sliced into rounds

2 courgettes (zucchini), roughly diced

8 green beans, roughly chopped

2 garlic cloves, crushed

1 x 400g (14oz) can of good-quality chopped tomatoes

1 x 400g (14oz) can of cannellini beans, drained and rinsed

500ml (2 cups) hot vegetable stock

1 sprig of fresh rosemary

1 sprig of fresh thyme

pinch of freshly grated nutmeg

handful of flat-leaf parsley, finely chopped

generous pinch each of sea salt and black pepper

Ladle this French-inspired stew into warmed bowls for a fresh and warming spring supper. Feel free to add in extra greens such as asparagus, shredded kale and podded broad beans, if you have them to hand. Serve with crusty bread for dipping, spread thickly with vegan butter, and a large glass of white wine.

1 Heat the oil in a large pan, add the leek, celery and carrot and cook over a medium-high heat for 5 minutes, stirring frequently to avoid sticking. Throw in the courgettes, green beans and garlic and cook for a further 2 minutes.

2 Pour in the chopped tomatoes, cannellini beans and vegetable stock and stir through. Add the rosemary and thyme sprigs, then simmer for 30 minutes.

3 Remove from the heat and discard the woody herbs. Stir through a pinch of nutmeg and season to taste with sea salt and plenty of black pepper. Scatter over the flat-leaf parsley just before serving.

EASY TIP

Pot au feu translates to 'pot on the fire'; this traditional one-pot meal is easily cooked on the hob, for a comforting, fuss-free supper.

Rustic hot pot

SERVES 4

Suitable for freezing

2 large baking potatoes, thinly sliced to about 3mm (⅛in)

2 tbsp sunflower oil

1 onion, finely diced

1 celery stick, finely diced

1 large carrot, peeled and thinly sliced into half-rounds

1 tsp dried sage

generous glug of red wine (ensure vegan)

1 x 400g (14oz) can of chopped tomatoes

1 x 400g (14oz) can of green lentils, drained and rinsed

2 leaves of savoy cabbage, roughly shredded

generous pinch each of sea salt and black pepper

Who doesn't love a slow-cooked hot pot? Often, however, time doesn't allow for slow-cooking, so here's my speedy version of this British classic. The trick? Cook the potato slices separately in the oven while you simmer the flavoursome filling. Best cooked in a cast-iron pot, then served at the table for everyone to help themselves. Serve with some freshly steamed greens, if you like.

1 Preheat the oven to 200°C/400°F/gas mark 6 and line two large baking trays with baking parchment.

2 Arrange the potato slices on the baking trays, ensuring the slices don't overlap. Use a pastry brush to brush a tablespoon of the oil over the potatoes, then bake in the oven for 20–22 minutes until the edges are golden.

3 Meanwhile, heat the remaining tablespoon of sunflower oil in a flameproof casserole dish or pan and throw in the onion, celery, carrot and sage. Cook over a medium-high heat for 2–3 minutes until the onion begins to soften, then pour in the wine. Reduce for a couple of minutes.

4 Pour in the chopped tomatoes, lentils and shredded cabbage, then simmer for 20 minutes, stirring frequently to avoid sticking. Season to taste with salt and pepper, then remove from the heat.

5 Carefully remove the sliced potatoes from the oven, and layer them over the hot pot filling. Serve hot.

EASY TIP

There's no need to peel the potatoes, simply scrub clean and leave the skin intact, for an overall rustic look with extra flavour.

Cottage pie stuffed potatoes

SERVES 4

4 large baking potatoes, scrubbed clean

2 tbsp sunflower oil

1 onion, finely diced

1 carrot, peeled and diced

1 x 400g (14oz) can of green lentils, drained and rinsed

4 rounded tbsp vegan cream cheese with herbs

generous pinch each of sea salt and black pepper

If you've become bored of the usual vegan cottage pie recipes, give the classic a twist with these stuffed potatoes. Serve with freshly steamed greens and cider-battered onion rings (page 292).

1 Preheat the oven to 200°C/400°F/gas mark 6.

2 Pierce the potatoes with a fork a few times, then rub with 1 tablespoon sunflower oil. Wrap each potato in foil, then bake in the oven for 1½ hours until softened.

3 Meanwhile, heat the remaining oil in a pan, then cook the onion for 5 minutes until it begins to soften and become golden. Add the carrot and lentils and cook for a further 2–3 minutes, before setting the pan aside.

4 Remove the potatoes from the oven and fold back the foil. Halve each potato, then leave until cool enough to handle. Scoop out the flesh from each potato half, leaving about 5mm (¼in) remaining near the potato skin. Add the potato flesh to the pan with the onion, carrot and lentils.

5 Stir the vegan cream cheese with herbs into the pan until the onion, carrot, lentils and potato are creamy. Season to taste with sea salt and black pepper.

6 Load each potato skin with the mix, then place the stuffed potatoes onto a baking tray lined with baking parchment. Return to the oven for 20–25 minutes until the tops are golden.

EASY TIP

Vegan cream cheese flavoured with herbs is available in most large supermarkets; however, if you don't have any to hand, simply add a teaspoon of dried mixed herbs along with mild vegan cream cheese.

Aubergine, orzo and olive traybake

SERVES 2 GENEROUSLY

*Suitable for freezing
(before adding the yogurt)*

1 tbsp rose harissa paste

1 tbsp sunflower oil

1 large aubergine (eggplant),
sliced into wedges

500g (2 cups/17oz) passata
(sieved tomatoes)

1 x 400g (14oz) can of chickpeas
(garbanzo beans), drained and
rinsed

4 tbsp dried orzo pasta (ensure
egg-free)

handful of pitted green olives

1 tsp dried oregano

pinch of ground cinnamon

juice of ¼ unwaxed lemon

small handful of flat-leaf parsley,
finely chopped

seeds of 1 pomegranate

2 tbsp unsweetened soya
yogurt

generous pinch each of sea salt
and black pepper

**This traybake works beautifully as a midweek meal, or
can easily be scaled up and served to special guests
for an impressive dish which is simple to cook, without
compromising on flavour. Delicious served with warm,
crusty bread, or with winter tabbouleh (page 99).**

1 Preheat the oven to 200°C/400°F/gas mark 6.

2 In a small bowl, whisk together the harissa and
sunflower oil. Brush the mix onto the aubergine wedges
and place them into a large, deep roasting tray. Roast in
the oven for 15 minutes.

3 Carefully remove the tray from the oven, then pour the
passata around the aubergine wedges, without covering
them. Stir in the chickpeas, orzo pasta, olives, oregano and
cinnamon. Loosely cover with foil and return the tray to
the oven for 30 minutes.

4 Remove the tray from the oven and squeeze over the
lemon juice. Season with a little sea salt and black pepper,
then scatter over the flat-leaf parsley and pomegranate
seeds. Spoon over the soya yogurt just before serving.

EASY TIP

Serve leftovers as a cold salad the following day: simply
toss through some peppery rocket (arugula) leaves and
refresh with a squeeze of lemon juice.

POT · POT ·
POT
1
POT · POT ·

Moroccan chickpea and squash traybake

SERVES 2

Suitable for freezing

500g (2 cups/17oz) passata (sieved tomatoes)

1 x 400g (14oz) can of chickpeas (garbanzo beans), drained and rinsed

2 tbsp sunflower oil

2 tsp rose harissa paste

1 tsp ground cumin

pinch of ground cinnamon

1 small butternut squash, peeled, deseeded and diced into bite-sized chunks

2 carrots, peeled and chopped

2 red onions, peeled and quartered

4 dried apricots, roughly chopped

juice of ½ unwaxed lemon

handful of flat-leaf parsley, chopped

handful of shelled pistachios, roughly chopped

generous pinch each of sea salt and black pepper

All the flavours of the Middle East, with little effort! This traybake is simple, filling and hearty, packed with chickpeas, apricots and pistachios. Serve with toasted pittas and a bowl of smooth houmous.

1 Preheat the oven to 180°C/350°F/gas mark 4.

2 Pour the passata and chickpeas into a large, deep roasting tray.

3 In a large bowl, stir together the oil, harissa, cumin and cinnamon. Stir in the butternut squash, carrots, red onions and dried apricots, ensuring they are coated in the spice mix. Spoon the vegetables into the roasting tray, over the chickpeas, spooning in any excess spice mix from the bowl.

4 Roast in the oven (uncovered) for 45–50 minutes until the butternut squash is tender.

5 Remove from the oven and stir through the lemon juice. Scatter over the parsley and pistachios, then season with sea salt and black pepper.

EASY TIP

Frozen butternut squash also works well in this recipe, saving you time and effort. Simply cook from frozen for the same amount of time.

Smoky baked bean pot pies

SERVES 4

1 sheet of ready-rolled puff
pastry (ensure dairy-free)

1 tbsp sunflower oil

1 red (bell) pepper, deseeded
and thinly sliced

1 tsp smoked paprika

2 x 400g (14oz) cans of baked
beans in tomato sauce

2 tbsp barbecue sauce (ensure
vegan)

generous pinch of sea salt

**A favourite with all ages, these easy 'cheat' pies are
quick and comforting, using store cupboard ingredients.
You'll just need 4 small, deep pie dishes. Cooking the
puff pastry lids separately to the filling means these pies
are ready in under 30 minutes. Serve with sweet potato
fries, if you like.**

1 Preheat the oven to 200°C/400°F/gas mark 6 and line
a baking tray with baking parchment.

2 Lay the pastry sheet out on a clean surface and cut out
4 pastry lids using the pie dishes as a guide. Place the lids
on the baking tray, then bake in the oven for 12–15 minutes
until golden and risen.

3 Meanwhile, heat the oil in a large pan and add the sliced
pepper. Cook over a medium heat for 4–5 minutes until
softened. Sprinkle in the smoked paprika and stir.

4 Stir in the baked beans and barbecue sauce, then
season to taste with sea salt. Spoon the bean filling into
the pie dishes, then bake in the oven for 5–10 minutes (this
heats the pie dishes, so the filling doesn't become cold
before serving).

5 Remove the pastry lids and the pie dishes from the
oven. Place the lids over the pie fillings and serve hot.

EASY TIP

I love making individual pot pies using small, deep pie
dishes but feel free to make one large pie, and serve it
family-style.

Roasted fajitas

SERVES 4

1 red (bell) pepper, deseeded and roughly sliced

1 yellow (bell) pepper, deseeded and roughly sliced

1 orange (bell) pepper, deseeded and roughly sliced

2 red onions, thinly sliced

2 tbsp sunflower oil

2 tsp fajita seasoning

1 tsp smoked paprika

small handful of coriander (cilantro) leaves, torn

juice of ½ unwaxed lemon

4 large white tortilla wraps

1 avocado, stoned, peeled and sliced

1 baby gem lettuce, quartered and core discarded

generous pinch each of smoked sea salt and black pepper

Throw your ingredients into a roasting tray and let the oven do the hard work. Peppers and red onion are gently roasted with Mexican-inspired spices, with minimal effort from you, then wrapped in soft tortillas with avocado and crisp baby gem lettuce.

1 Preheat the oven to 200°C/400°F/gas mark 6.

2 Arrange the sliced peppers and red onion in a deep roasting tray.

3 In a small bowl, mix together the oil, fajita seasoning and smoked paprika, then drizzle over the vegetables. Turn the vegetables to ensure they are all coated in the spiced oil. Roast in the oven for 25 minutes.

4 Carefully remove the roasting tray from the oven and season with salt and pepper. Scatter over the coriander leaves and stir through the lime juice.

5 Lay out the tortilla wraps and fill each with avocado slices and baby gem lettuce. Liberally spoon in the baked filling and fold into fajitas.

EASY TIP

Found in most supermarkets, fajita seasoning is a pre-mixed spice blend that saves you the time and effort of mixing the individual herbs and spices!

Speedy chickpea burgers

SERVES 2

1 x 400g (14oz) can of chickpeas (garbanzo beans), drained and rinsed, refrigerated until chilled

2 tsp ground cumin

1 tsp smoked paprika

1 tsp rose harissa paste

generous handful of flat-leaf parsley, including stalks

generous handful of coriander (cilantro), including stalks

1 thick slice of day-old white bread, grated into fine breadcrumbs

1 tbsp sunflower seeds

4 tbsp sunflower oil

2 white seeded bread buns, toasted

2 heaped tsp vegan mayo

2 handfuls of wild rocket (arugula) leaves

8 thin red onion rings

generous pinch of salt

When the need for a burger arises, it arises fast. Enter the 15-minute burger! This go-to recipe is quick, simple and satisfying. The burger mix is suitable for freezing: simply defrost, shape and fry lightly for fresh burgers with even less effort. Serve with burger sauce (page 308) or tangy mustard and apple slaw (page 279).

1 Add the chickpeas, cumin, smoked paprika, harissa, parsley and coriander to a high-powered blender or food processor and blitz until semi-smooth. A few chunks means extra bite!

2 Carefully remove the mixture from the blender and shape into two flat burgers.

3 Mix together the breadcrumbs and sunflower seeds on a plate, then press the burgers into the mix, coating on all sides.

4 Heat the oil in a frying pan over a medium-high heat until hot. Carefully place the burgers in the pan and cook for 4–5 minutes on each side until golden.

5 Arrange the toasted bread buns on plates. Place the cooked chickpea burgers into the buns, then top with vegan mayo and load over the rocket and red onion.

EASY TIP
Keeping the chickpeas refrigerated before use gives your burgers a firmer texture.

Go-to soy, lime and peanut stir-fry

SERVES 2 GENEROUSLY

1 tbsp sunflower oil

10 florets of Tenderstem broccoli

1 large carrot, peeled and finely chopped

1 red (bell) pepper, deseeded and thinly sliced

½ tsp dried chilli flakes

4 leaves of cavolo nero, shredded (tough stems removed)

8 sugarsnap peas, halved diagonally

2 tbsp light soy sauce

juice of ½ unwaxed lime

2 spring onions (scallions), finely chopped

small handful of coriander (cilantro), roughly torn

2 tbsp salted peanuts, roughly chopped

As the title suggests, this is one of my go-to recipes, when I need something quick, tasty and nourishing. There's no need for a separate sauce as the chilli flakes, soy sauce and fresh lime juice deliver on flavour. Serve with tofu-fried rice (page 185).

1 Heat the oil in a wok over a high heat. Throw in the broccoli, carrot, pepper and chilli flakes and stir-fry for 2–3 minutes. Add the cavolo nero and sugarsnap peas and stir-fry for a further minute.

2 Stir in the soy sauce and cook for 2 minutes, stirring constantly until it reduces.

3 Remove from the heat and squeeze through the lime juice. Scatter with spring onions, coriander and chopped salted peanuts.

EASY TIP

These vegetables are all suitable for quick-cooking, making this stir-fry ready in under 15 minutes. Other quick-cooked vegetables include green beans, small cauliflower florets, mushrooms and asparagus.

Korean barbecue jackfruit tacos

SERVES 2

1 tbsp sunflower oil

2 garlic cloves, crushed

1 tbsp soft light brown sugar

2 tbsp gochujang paste (see 'Easy Tip' below)

2 tbsp light soy sauce

1 tbsp tomato purée (paste)

1 x 400g (14oz) can of jackfruit, thoroughly drained and rinsed

1 tbsp sesame seeds

2 spring onions (scallions), finely chopped

¼ red cabbage, thinly sliced

4 radishes, thinly sliced

4 crisp taco shells

Satisfy all of your taste buds with these Korean-style tacos. In the perfect balance of sweet and salty, jackfruit is cooked in a rich sauce, for a chunky and meaty meal. I love this in crisp taco shells, but it is equally as delicious served in soft tortilla wraps or warmed bread buns.

1 In a large pan, heat the oil and garlic over a medium heat for 2 minutes until the garlic softens and becomes fragrant.

2 Stir in the sugar, gochujang paste, soy sauce and tomato purée with 2 tablespoons cold water, then add the jackfruit. Cook over a medium heat for 10 minutes, stirring frequently with a wooden spoon to gently break up the pieces of jackfruit into thin shreds.

3 Stir in the sesame seeds and spring onions, then remove from the heat.

4 Load red cabbage and sliced radishes into the taco shells and top with the Korean barbecue jackfruit. Serve hot.

EASY TIP

Gochujang paste or Korean chilli paste is a blend of spices, pepper, vinegar and sugar. It is available in large supermarkets in the world food aisle or with the prepared spice mixes.

Mac 'n' roots

SERVES 2 GENEROUSLY

*Suitable for freezing
(root vegetable sauce only)*

3 carrots, peeled and roughly chopped

1 large baking potato, peeled and roughly chopped

½ butternut squash, peeled, deseeded and roughly chopped

200g (2 cups) dried macaroni (ensure egg-free)

1 tsp dried sage

200ml (generous ¾ cup) unsweetened soya milk

generous handful of fresh chives, finely chopped

generous pinch each of sea salt and black pepper

When your store cupboards look depleted, this simple dish of macaroni and creamed root vegetables will come to the rescue, using simple ingredients and vegetables that are just past their best. For me, this is delicious without the addition of vegan cheese, but feel free to sprinkle some on if you wish. Don't forgo the fresh chives: they add a creamy, mildly oniony flavour to the sauce that is simply delicious.

1 Bring a large pan of water to the boil over a medium heat, then throw in the chopped carrots, potato and butternut squash. Simmer for 20 minutes until the vegetables have softened, then drain.

2 Meanwhile, bring another pan of water to the boil and add in the macaroni. Cook for 10–12 minutes until *al dente*, then drain. Return the cooked macaroni to the pan.

3 Transfer the cooked carrot, potato and butternut squash to a high-powered jug blender jug and add the sage. Pour in the soya milk and blitz until completely smooth.

4 Pour the sauce over the macaroni and stir through over a medium heat.

5 Remove from the heat and stir in the chives. Season to taste with salt and pepper. Serve hot.

EASY TIP

Frozen butternut squash works really well in this recipe. Throw into the pan with the carrots and potato to cook from frozen.

Baked Caribbean sweet potato with rice 'n' beans

SERVES 2 GENEROUSLY

2 sweet potatoes, peeled and diced into even, bite-sized chunks

1 red (bell) pepper, deseeded and thinly sliced

4 tbsp white basmati rice

1 x 400g (14oz) can of red kidney beans, drained and rinsed

1 x 400ml (14fl oz) can of full-fat coconut milk

2 tsp jerk seasoning

juice of ½ unwaxed lime

2 spring onions (scallions), finely chopped

handful of flat-leaf parsley, roughly chopped

generous pinch each of sea salt and black pepper

Enjoy a taste of the Caribbean with this simple, 'throw-it-all-in' supper. Add the ingredients to the tray and bake in the oven while you sip on a fruity cocktail and dream about long summer days.

1 Preheat the oven to 200°C/400°F/gas mark 6.

2 Throw the sweet potatoes, red pepper, rice and kidney beans into a deep roasting tray. Stir through the coconut milk and jerk seasoning, then loosely cover the tray with foil. Bake in the oven for 40–45 minutes until the potatoes are tender and the rice is plump.

3 Carefully remove from the oven and discard the foil. Stir through the lime juice and spring onions, then scatter with flat-leaf parsley. Season with salt and pepper.

EASY TIP

Jerk seasoning is a blend of chillies, thyme, nutmeg and cinnamon and gives a Jamaican flavour to any dish. You'll find it in the spice aisle of most supermarkets.

Budget kidney bean curry

SERVES 2 GENEROUSLY

Suitable for freezing

1 tbsp sunflower oil

1 onion, diced

1 garlic clove, crushed

1 red (bell) pepper, deseeded and thinly sliced

1 tsp ground cumin

1 tsp ground turmeric

1 rounded tbsp medium curry paste (ensure dairy-free)

1 x 400g (14oz) can of chopped tomatoes

1 x 400g (14oz) can of red kidney beans, drained and rinsed

handful of spinach leaves

small handful of coriander (cilantro) leaves, roughly torn

generous pinch of sea salt

Kidney beans are often associated with chillies and other Mexican dishes, but they make a wonderful addition to an Indian-style curry. This wallet-friendly version of the classic dish *rajma* uses store cupboard ingredients alongside some fresh ingredients to create a mouth-watering supper. I love to serve this with vegan naan bread, for dipping.

1 Add the oil and onion to a large pan and cook over a medium-high heat for 2–3 minutes until softened and fragrant. Add the garlic, red pepper, cumin, turmeric and curry paste and cook for a further minute, stirring constantly to avoid sticking.

2 Pour in the chopped tomatoes and kidney beans and cook for 8 minutes. Stir through the spinach leaves and cook for a further 2 minutes.

3 Remove from the heat and scatter with coriander. Season to taste with sea salt.

EASY TIP

Choose a versatile medium-strength curry paste, but ensure it is dairy-free. Then add in extra spices from your store cupboard to personalize your supper!

Easiest ever dhal

SERVES 4

Suitable for freezing

300g (1½ cups) dried red lentils

2 tbsp medium curry paste
(ensure dairy-free)

pinch of ground turmeric

pinch of ground cumin

pinch of dried chilli flakes

1 litre (4 cups) hot vegetable
stock

1 x 400ml (14fl oz) can of full-fat
coconut milk

zest and juice of 1 unwaxed lime

2 tbsp coconut yogurt

generous pinch of sea salt

I love dhal, delicately spiced and oh-so comforting.
Over the years I've simplified my favourite dhal recipe
(mainly due to being too hungry, or too lazy to wait for it
to cook!). I hope you love this 30-minute, one-pot recipe
too! Top with cheat's pink pickled onions (page 279) for
a tangy, colourful finish.

1 Add the lentils to a large pan, along with the curry
paste, turmeric, cumin, chilli flakes and vegetable
stock. Bring to the boil over a high heat, then simmer
for 20 minutes, stirring frequently.

2 Pour in the coconut milk and cook for a further
5–6 minutes, stirring constantly, until the lentils break
down and become creamy.

3 Remove from the heat and stir through the lime zest
and juice. Season to taste with sea salt, then stir through
the coconut yogurt.

EASY TIP
Use this as a basic recipe for dhal variations, including
adding carrot and coriander, caramelized onions or
spinach. Let your flavour imagination run wild!

Cauliflower korma with sultanas

SERVES 4

Suitable for freezing

1 tbsp sunflower oil

1 onion, finely diced

1 large cauliflower, broken into bite-sized florets

1 garlic clove, crushed

1 tsp ground turmeric

1 tsp ground cumin

1 rounded tbsp mild curry paste (ensure dairy-free)

1 x 400ml (14fl oz) can of full-fat coconut milk

1 x 400g (14oz) can of green lentils, drained and rinsed

small handful of sultanas (golden raisins)

juice of 1 unwaxed lemon

2 rounded tbsp coconut yogurt

small handful of coriander (cilantro), roughly torn

generous pinch of sea salt

It's no secret that this recipe is a regular in my kitchen – I love whipping up this creamy curry once a week! I tend to have the basic ingredients in the store cupboard and cauliflower is the perfect korma companion, ready to soak up all those lovely flavours of spices, coconut yogurt and coriander. Serve with easy pilau rice (page 300).

1 Heat the oil in a large pan, add the onion and cauliflower and cook over a medium-high heat for 3–4 minutes, stirring frequently to avoid sticking. Stir in the garlic, turmeric, cumin and curry paste and cook for a further minute.

2 Pour in the coconut milk and green lentils, then loosely place a lid over the pan. Cook for 20 minutes, stirring occasionally.

3 Remove from the heat and stir through the sultanas. Squeeze in the lemon juice and season to taste with sea salt. Stir through the coconut yogurt, then scatter over the coriander just before serving.

EASY TIP

Sultanas add a pop of sweetness to the korma, but if you don't want to use them, or if your store cupboard is depleted, replace with a generous tablespoon of mango chutney.

Easy biryani

SERVES 4

1 tbsp sunflower oil

1 onion, diced

1 red (bell) pepper, deseeded and thinly sliced

½ cauliflower, broken into small florets

6 florets of Tenderstem broccoli

10 green beans, halved

2 garlic cloves, crushed

1 tsp ground turmeric

1 tsp ground cumin

pinch of dried chilli flakes

1 tbsp medium curry powder (ensure dairy-free)

400g (2 cups) white basmati rice

1 litre (4 cups) hot vegetable stock

handful of roasted and salted cashews

juice of 1 unwaxed lemon

small handful of coriander (cilantro) leaves, roughly torn

generous pinch each of sea salt and black pepper

This colourful rice dish is cooked in one pot (meaning less washing up) and is ready in just 15 minutes. I love the combination of cauliflower, broccoli and green beans in this recipe, but feel free to switch up to what you have available. Serve with a spoonful of cooling coconut yogurt.

1 In a large pan, heat the oil and onion over a high heat for 1 minute until the onion begins to soften. Throw in the red pepper, cauliflower, broccoli, green beans and garlic and cook for 2–3 minutes, stirring constantly to avoid sticking. Add all the spices and cook for a further minute.

2 Stir in the rice and vegetable stock and loosely place a lid over the pan. Cook for 10 minutes, stirring frequently, until the rice is plump and softened.

3 Remove from the heat and stir through the cashews, lemon juice, sea salt and black pepper. Scatter with coriander leaves just before serving.

EASY TIP
White basmati rice offers the quickest cooking time for this speedy biryani. Brown basmati rice has a nuttier flavour and higher fibre content, but requires a longer cooking time of around 30 minutes.

Piri piri pilaf

SERVES 4

---

1 tbsp sunflower oil

1 large sweet potato, peeled and diced into 1cm (½in) pieces

1 red onion, thinly sliced

1 red (bell) pepper, deseeded and thinly sliced

1 yellow (bell) pepper, deseeded and thinly sliced

1 garlic clove, crushed

1 heaped tbsp piri piri seasoning

pinch of ground turmeric

1 x 400g (14oz) can of red kidney beans, drained and rinsed

250g (1¼ cups) basmati rice

200ml (generous ¾ cup) fresh orange juice

400ml (generous 1½ cups) vegetable stock

large handful of flat-leaf parsley (about 30g/1oz), finely chopped

juice of 1 unwaxed lemon

1 small red chilli, deseeded and finely chopped

generous pinch each of sea salt and black pepper

All of the family will love this Portuguese-style pilaf, loaded with sweet potato, peppers, red onion and spicy piri piri flavours, with a hit of orange and lemon. This all-in-one dinner is perfect bowl food, but feel free to serve it with a cooling cucumber salad. Adjust the red chilli to suit more delicate palates, or leave out completely, if you prefer.

1 In a large pan, heat the oil and sweet potato over a high heat for 2–3 minutes. Throw in the onion, peppers, garlic, piri piri seasoning and turmeric and cook for a further 2 minutes, stirring constantly to avoid sticking.

2 Stir in the kidney beans and basmati rice, then pour in the orange juice and vegetable stock. Reduce the heat to medium and cook for 15 minutes, stirring frequently. When all of the liquid has been absorbed, remove the pan from the heat. Cover the pan securely with a lid and allow to stand for 5 minutes until the rice is tender.

3 Stir through the chopped parsley and lemon juice until combined. Season to taste with salt and pepper, then scatter with red chilli.

EASY TIP

Piri piri seasoning is found in most supermarkets. It is a blend of chillies, thyme, garlic and dried lemon peel, saving you time mixing up your own!

Something Special

Tomato and olive tarte tatin

SERVES 4

1 sheet of prepared puff pastry (ensure dairy-free)

1 tbsp sunflower oil

500g (1lb 2oz) mixed baby tomatoes

½ red onion, thinly sliced

2 tsp balsamic vinegar

100g (3½oz) pitted black olives

1 sprig of fresh thyme, leaves picked and finely chopped

generous pinch of black pepper

Make this impressive tarte tatin for a barbecue, garden party or picnic for a summery taste of the Mediterranean. Not only does the tarte tatin look wonderful, but it's simple and quick to prepare, which means more time enjoying the summer, and less time in the kitchen!

1 Lay the pastry sheet out on a clean, dry surface and place a large ovenproof frying pan over the top. Cut around the pan, leaving an extra 2cm (¾in) border. Prick the pastry with a fork, then set aside.

2 Preheat the oven to 180°C/350°F/gas mark 4.

3 Add the sunflower oil to the ovenproof pan and throw in the tomatoes and red onion. Cook for 2 minutes over a medium-high heat, then drizzle in the balsamic vinegar. Reduce down for 8 minutes then remove from the heat. Stir in the olives and chopped thyme. Season with lots of black pepper.

4 Place the pastry on top of the cooked tomatoes in the pan, pricked side downwards, and carefully tuck the edges under the tomatoes. Bake in the oven for 20 minutes until the pastry is golden. Allow the pan to cool for a few moments before carefully turning out onto a serving plate.

EASY TIP

Red, orange and yellow tomatoes give a colourful, summery appearance to the dish, but if you only have baby red (cherry or mini plum) tomatoes available, it will not take away from the flavour.

Roasted pumpkin gnocchi

SERVES 4

Suitable for freezing

1 medium pumpkin, tough skin and seeds removed, flesh roughly sliced

2 tsp dried sage

drizzle of sunflower oil

6 leaves of cavolo nero, roughly shredded and tough stem discarded

500g (1lb 2oz) gnocchi (ensure vegan)

400ml (generous 1½ cups) hot vegetable stock

generous pinch each of sea salt and black pepper

Don't let that Halloween pumpkin go to waste! Whip up this autumnal gnocchi dish, with sage and dark cavolo nero that is as comforting as it is delicious. The recipe also works well with seasonal roasted butternut squash. Serve in warmed bowls (cosy jumpers optional).

1 Preheat the oven to 180°C/350°F/gas mark 4.

2 Arrange the pumpkin over a couple of baking trays and sprinkle with the sage. Drizzle over a little sunflower oil, then roast in the oven for 25–30 minutes until softened.

3 Meanwhile, bring a large pan of water to the boil and add the cavolo nero and gnocchi. Cook for 3 minutes, then thoroughly drain.

4 Remove the roasted pumpkin from the oven and spoon three-quarters of it into a high-powered blender jug. Pour in the hot vegetable stock then blitz on high until silky smooth. Pour the sauce into the pan, stirring it through the cooked gnocchi and kale.

5 Spoon the remaining pumpkin into the pan and lightly stir. Season to taste with sea salt and plenty of black pepper.

EASY TIP

Ready-made gnocchi can be found in supermarkets, and is a great addition to any store cupboard for fast and filling meals. Do ensure that the gnocchi is vegan, as some brands add eggs or milk proteins.

Asparagus cream linguine

SERVES 2

200g (7oz) dried linguine (ensure egg-free)

1 tbsp sunflower oil

2 garlic cloves, crushed

6 asparagus spears, roughly chopped and woody ends discarded

small glug of white wine (ensure vegan)

200ml (generous ¾ cup) soya single (light) cream

handful of small basil leaves

generous pinch each of sea salt and black pepper

Will you be my Valentine? A bowl of this creamy, luxurious linguine will impress your significant other (or soon to be significant other), despite the minimal effort that goes into making it. I won't tell if you don't...

1 Bring a pan of salted water to the boil, then add in the linguine. Cook for 8–10 minutes until *al dente*, then drain thoroughly.

2 Meanwhile, heat the oil, garlic and asparagus in a frying pan over a medium heat for 2–3 minutes until the asparagus starts to soften and become brighter in colour. Pour in the white wine and reduce for 2 minutes.

3 Stir in the soya cream, then simmer for 5 minutes. Season to taste with sea salt and plenty of black pepper.

4 Add the pasta to the sauce and stir to coat fully. Serve in warmed dishes, scattered with basil leaves.

EASY TIP

If you're really pushing the boat out, drizzle with a little truffle oil, or simply grate over some vegan parmesan for the cheese lover in your life.

Open lasagne verde

SERVES 2

4 dried pasta sheets (ensure egg-free)

2 tbsp sunflower oil

1 leek, finely chopped

1 courgette (zucchini), finely chopped

2 generous handfuls of fresh spinach

1 garlic clove, crushed

small handful of pine nuts

handful of frozen peas

4 rounded tbsp vegan cream cheese

handful of small basil leaves

generous pinch each of sea salt and black pepper

Treat an unexpected guest to a lunch to remember – and it only takes 15 minutes to cook! Elegant, simple and fresh, what's not to love about this twist on a classic? Serve with a leafy side salad and slices of garlic baguette, if you wish.

1 Bring a large pan of water to the boil, then stir in 1 tablespoon of the sunflower oil before adding the pasta sheets. Cook for 8–10 minutes until *al dente*, then drain away the water.

2 In a frying pan, heat the remaining oil, leek and courgette for 3–4 minutes over a medium-high heat until the leek begins to soften. Add the spinach, garlic, pine nuts and frozen peas, then cook for a further 3–4 minutes, stirring constantly. Spoon in the vegan cream cheese and stir to distribute. Season to taste with sea salt and plenty of black pepper.

3 Place one cooked lasagne sheet on a serving plate and load on a quarter of the green lasagne filling. Place a second lasagne sheet over this, then spoon over another quarter of the filling. Repeat for the second open lasagne.

EASY TIP

Adding a tablespoon of sunflower oil to the pasta cooking water prevents the pasta sheets from sticking together.

Butternut squash, caramelized onion and hazelnut galette

SERVES 4

2 tbsp sunflower oil

1 red onion, sliced

1 small butternut squash, peeled, deseeded and thinly sliced into even wedges

1 tbsp blanched hazelnuts, roughly chopped

1 sheet of ready-rolled shortcrust pastry (ensure dairy-free), at room temperature

generous pinch of fennel seeds

generous pinch each of sea salt and black pepper

This galette is made for sharing. If you're a little nervous about cooking with pastry, rest assured that the rustic appearance of this freeform pie will hide any mistakes! Serve with a leafy green salad and crisp green apples.

1 Heat the oil in a large frying pan, add the red onion and butternut squash and cook over a medium heat for 10 minutes, stirring frequently to avoid sticking. When the butternut squash appears tender, remove from the heat and stir through the hazelnuts.

2 Preheat the oven to 180°C/350°F/gas mark 4 and line a baking sheet with baking parchment.

3 Lay the pastry on the lined baking sheet, then trim the corners to form a rough circle.

4 Spoon the cooked onion, butternut squash and hazelnuts into the centre of the pastry, leaving a 4cm (1½in) border at the edges and piling the vegetables a little higher in the centre of the pastry. Fold the edge of the pastry inwards, encasing some of the vegetables, but leaving the vegetables in the centre exposed. Allow the pastry to overlap in folds to create a rustic shape.

5 Press the fennel seeds into the exposed pastry, then bake in the oven for 25–30 minutes until the pastry is golden. Allow to stand for 5 minutes before slicing.

EASY TIP

Many brands of prepared shortcrust pastry are vegan, as they are made with vegetable oil instead of dairy butter, but always check the label before you buy. Store in the fridge, but bring to room temperature 30 minutes before using to avoid any cracks in the pastry.

Cashews and broccoli in plum sauce

SERVES 4

Suitable for freezing

For the plum sauce

6 ripe plums, stoned and roughly chopped

3 tbsp soft light brown sugar

2 tsp ginger purée

½ tsp dried chilli flakes

½ tsp Chinese five-spice

2 star anise

2 tbsp dark soy sauce

For the cashews and broccoli

2 tbsp sunflower oil

1 head of broccoli, broken into even florets

6 tbsp salted cashews

2 spring onions (scallions), finely chopped

small handful of coriander (cilantro) leaves, roughly torn

Celebrate Chinese New Year (or any Friday night in) with this sweet, savoury and nutty dish. The Eastern flavours will transport you to celebratory times, making it perfect for dinner with friends. Serve with tofu-fried rice (opposite).

1 To make the plum sauce, add the plums and brown sugar to a large pan set over a medium-high heat, then add the ginger purée, chilli flakes, Chinese five-spice and star anise. Simmer, stirring frequently to avoid catching. After 20 minutes, add 100ml (scant ½ cup) cold water, stir and simmer for a further 10 minutes. Remove from the heat then stir through the soy sauce. Discard the star anise, then use a stick blender to blitz the sauce until smooth and glossy.

2 Meanwhile, heat the oil in a large wok over a high heat. Throw in the broccoli and stir-fry for 2–3 minutes, then add the cashews and stir-fry for another minute.

3 Pour the smooth plum sauce into the wok and stir-fry for 1 minute until the broccoli and cashews are coated in the sauce. Remove from the heat and scatter over the spring onions and coriander. Serve hot.

EASY TIP

The versatile plum sauce is also delicious served over crisp tofu, as a dipping sauce for tempura, or as an alternative to cranberry sauce with any roast dinner.

Tofu-fried rice

SERVES 4

300g (1½ cups) white basmati rice

1 tbsp sunflower oil

280g (9oz) block of extra-firm tofu, drained of excess water (see 'Easy Tip' below)

pinch of ground turmeric

2cm (¾in) piece of ginger, grated

1 garlic clove, crushed

2 carrots, peeled and grated

handful of frozen peas

2 tbsp dark soy sauce

2 spring onions (scallions), finely chopped

generous handful of coriander (cilantro), roughly torn

This impressive alternative to egg-fried rice is the perfect dish for any celebration, particularly around Chinese New Year. The recipe works well with rice that has been cooked and cooled, but if you don't have time to wait, simply rinse the cooked rice in cold tap water before adding to the pan. Serve with cashews and broccoli in plum sauce (opposite).

1 Add the rice to a pan and cover with 450ml (scant 2 cups) boiling water. Bring to the boil, then cover and simmer for 10–12 minutes until the water has been absorbed and the rice is fluffy. Remove from the heat then rinse with plenty of cold water to help the rice cool down, then drain thoroughly.

2 Meanwhile, heat the oil in a wok over a high heat. Break the tofu into small pieces with a fork, then throw into the wok and stir-fry for 2 minutes. Add in the turmeric and ginger and stir-fry for a further 2 minutes.

3 Add the garlic, carrots, peas and soy sauce, along with the cooked and cooled rice, then stir-fry for 2–3 minutes.

4 Remove from the heat and stir in the spring onions and coriander.

EASY TIP

There's no need to press the tofu for this recipe, simply drain of excess water by blotting with kitchen paper or with a clean, dry cloth.

Sticky pineapple massaman

SERVES 4

2 tbsp sunflower oil

1 small pineapple, tough skin and core discarded, flesh chopped into 3cm (1¼in) pieces

1 red onion, thinly sliced

1 carrot, peeled and sliced into thin matchsticks

2 garlic cloves, crushed

2cm (¾in) piece of ginger, grated

pinch of dried chilli flakes

1 tsp ground cumin

½ tsp ground cinnamon

½ tsp ground cardamom

½ tsp grated nutmeg

1 rounded tbsp Thai red curry paste (ensure vegan)

2 tbsp smooth peanut butter

2 x 400ml (14fl oz) cans of full-fat coconut milk

1 tbsp light soy sauce

2 bay leaves

8 sugarsnap peas, sliced diagonally

juice of 1 unwaxed lime

1 tbsp roasted and salted peanuts, roughly chopped

handful of coriander (cilantro), roughly torn

Make it a curry night to remember with this fusion dish. Caramelized pineapple is the star of the show, in a fragrant peanut and coconut sauce.

1 Heat 1 tablespoon of the oil in a large pan over a high heat and add the chopped pineapple. Cook for 5–6 minutes, tossing the pan regularly until the pineapple starts to caramelize. Spoon the pineapple into a bowl and set aside, then return the pan to the hob.

2 Heat the remaining tablespoon of oil in the pan over a medium-high heat and throw in the onion, carrot, garlic and ginger. Cook for 2 minutes, then stir in the chilli flakes, cumin, cinnamon, cardamom and nutmeg. Cook for 1 further minute until fragrant.

3 Stir through the curry paste and peanut butter, then pour in the coconut milk. Stir in the soy sauce and add the bay leaves. Simmer for 30 minutes, stirring frequently to avoid sticking.

4 Throw in the sugarsnap peas and caramelized pineapple and cook for a further 2 minutes.

5 Remove from the heat and stir in the lime juice. Scatter with chopped peanuts and coriander just before serving.

EASY TIP

Adding additional spices including cinnamon, cardamom, nutmeg and cumin transforms a Thai red curry paste into something really special.

Tahini-roasted cauliflower with lemon and thyme

SERVES 4

2 tbsp sunflower oil

4 rounded tbsp good-quality tahini

1 tsp smoked paprika

1 tsp ras el hanout

½ tsp ground cinnamon

juice of ½ unwaxed lemon

2 sprigs of thyme, leaves picked and roughly chopped

1 medium cauliflower, leaves and stem discarded

1 x 400g (14oz) can of butterbeans, drained and rinsed

1 unwaxed lemon, sliced into wedges

handful of flat-leaf parsley, finely chopped

generous pinch of sea salt and black pepper

This Middle Eastern-spiced cauliflower makes the perfect centrepiece for any celebration. Creamy tahini is whisked with gentle spices including ras el hanout, which can be found in most supermarkets. Serve with herby stuffed cabbage leaves (page 295) and cheat's aioli (page 307).

1 Preheat the oven to 200°C/400°F/gas mark 6.

2 In a bowl, whisk together the oil with 3 tablespoons of the tahini. Whisk in the smoked paprika, ras el hanout and cinnamon and stir in the lemon juice and thyme to create a smooth sauce. Season with salt and pepper.

3 Dip the whole cauliflower into the sauce to coat it completely, then place the cauliflower in a large lidded casserole dish. Pour over any remaining sauce, then place on the lid. Bake in the oven for 45 minutes.

4 Carefully remove the dish from the oven and toss the butterbeans around the base of the cauliflower. Lay in the lemon wedges, then return to the oven without the lid for a further 15 minutes to roast until the cauliflower appears golden.

5 Remove from the oven and stir the flat-leaf parsley into the butterbeans. Use the remaining tablespoon of tahini to drizzle over the top of the roasted cauliflower.

EASY TIP

Ensure that the cauliflower fits in your casserole dish; the lid should not touch the top of the cauliflower.

Thai spiced no-fish pie

SERVES 4

1 tbsp sunflower oil, plus 1 tsp for brushing

4 spring onions (scallions), chopped

4 sugarsnap peas, sliced lengthways

1 red chilli, deseeded and finely chopped

handful of frozen or fresh edamame beans

1 tbsp Thai red curry paste (ensure vegan)

1 x 400ml (14fl oz) can of full-fat coconut milk

1 x 400g (14oz) can of jackfruit, thoroughly drained, rinsed and broken into strands

handful of dill, finely chopped

zest and juice of 1 unwaxed lime

4 sheets of filo pastry (ensure dairy-free)

Fresh, fragrant and comforting, this crispy topped pie uses jackfruit to replace flaked fish for a familiar texture and flavour. A perfect way to impress your guests! Serve with lightly steamed broccoli.

1 Preheat the oven to 180°C/350°F/gas mark 4.

2 In a large pan, heat the 1 tablespoon oil over a high heat then throw in the spring onions, sugarsnap peas, chilli and edamame beans. Stir-fry for 2 minutes. Stir in the curry paste, then pour in the coconut milk and jackfruit strands and simmer for 10 minutes.

3 Stir in the dill, lime zest and juice and transfer to a deep pie dish.

4 Tear the filo pastry sheets into pieces, then scrunch over the top of the pie filling, until it covers the top completely. Brush with 1 teaspoon sunflower oil and bake in the oven for 15–18 minutes until golden. Serve hot.

EASY TIP

Many brands of Thai red curry paste available in supermarkets are vegan, however do check the label as they can contain fish sauce or anchovies.

Warm jasmine rice, coconut and peanut salad with lime

SERVES 4

350g (1¾ cups) jasmine rice

4 rounded tbsp thick coconut yogurt

zest and juice of 1 unwaxed lime

4 spring onions (scallions), finely chopped

generous handful of roasted and salted peanuts, roughly chopped

This simple rice salad is rich with coconut yogurt, crunchy roasted peanuts and zesty lime and spring onions. A small dish of this makes for a satisfying weekend lunch, or as a side to any Thai-style stir-fried dish. Serve with steamed greens, including sugarsnap peas, Tenderstem broccoli and pak choi.

1 Add the rice to a large pan with 600ml (2½ cups) boiling water, then simmer over a medium heat for 15–20 minutes until the rice is tender. Drain thoroughly, fluff through with a fork and allow to stand for 5 minutes.

2 Stir in the coconut yogurt, lime zest and juice. Scatter with spring onions and peanuts.

EASY TIP

Jasmine rice has a balanced sweet flavour, which works well with the creamy coconut yogurt and acidic lime. Basmati rice will offer a similar sweetness and fragrance if you don't have jasmine rice available.

Hoisin no-duck pancakes

SERVES 4

Suitable for freezing

For the pancakes

150g (1¼ cups) plain (all-purpose) flour, plus extra for dusting

1 tsp sunflower oil

For the jackfruit no-duck

1 tbsp sunflower oil

2 garlic cloves, crushed

2 x 400g (14oz) cans of jackfruit, thoroughly drained, rinsed and broken into strands

1 tsp Chinese five-spice

4 tbsp hoisin sauce

1 tbsp light soy sauce

2 spring onions (scallions), finely chopped

1 tbsp sesame seeds

4cm (1½in) piece of cucumber, thinly sliced into matchsticks

cheat's pink pickles (page 279), to serve (optional)

Turn an ordinary supper into something special with these Chinese-style pancakes loaded with sticky hoisin jackfruit for a vegan-friendly alternative to duck.

1 To make the pancakes, add the flour to a bowl, then pour in 120ml (½ cup) boiling water. Stir together to form a thick dough, then allow the dough to rest for 10 minutes until it is cool enough for you to comfortably handle.

2 Lightly dust a clean work surface with flour, then knead the dough for 5 minutes. Cut the dough into 8 even pieces. Lightly dust a rolling pin with flour, then roll each piece as thinly as possible.

3 Use a pastry brush to brush a frying pan lightly with oil, then place over a medium-high heat. Carefully add each pancake to the pan, cooking for 30 seconds before flipping the pancake and cooking the other side for 30 seconds, ensuring they don't brown. Keep warm.

4 Heat the oil and garlic in a large frying pan for 1 minute until softened and fragrant. Add the jackfruit strands with the Chinese five-spice and stir-fry for 2–3 minutes.

5 Spoon in the hoisin sauce and soy sauce and stir-fry for 4–5 minutes until the sauce is bubbling.

6 Scatter over the spring onions and sesame, then spoon onto a serving platter, along with the sliced cucumber and pink pickles, ready to load into the warm pancakes.

EASY TIP

Hoisin is a sweet and salty sauce, made with fermented soya beans, but is made even tastier with added Chinese five-spice and soy sauce.

Miso mushrooms with sesame and soy

SERVES 2

1 tbsp sunflower oil

250g (2 cups) chestnut mushrooms, brushed clean and roughly sliced

100g (1½ cups) button mushrooms, brushed clean

3 tbsp sesame seeds

4 handfuls of shredded kale, tough stems removed

2 garlic cloves, crushed

1 tbsp white miso paste

2 tbsp light soy sauce

2 spring onions (scallions), thinly sliced

handful of flat-leaf parsley, finely chopped

This Japanese-style dish is easy to prepare, with simple mushrooms, garlic, sesame, kale and miso. Miso paste is made from fermented soya beans and has an umami, savoury flavour. Serve with rice or egg-free noodles.

1 Heat the oil in a wok over a medium-high heat, then throw in the chestnut and button mushrooms. Stir-fry for 3–4 minutes.

2 Add the sesame seeds, kale and garlic and stir-fry for a further minute.

3 Spoon in the miso paste and 2 tablespoons hot water and stir. Then add the soy sauce and cook down for 4–5 minutes, stirring frequently until the liquid reduces.

4 Remove from the heat and scatter with spring onions and chopped parsley.

EASY TIP

Miso paste can be found in most large supermarkets. White miso paste has a mild, savoury flavour which works perfectly with the earthy mushrooms.

Smoky yogurt-marinated mushroom and aubergine skewers

SERVES 4

5 rounded tbsp plain soya yogurt

1 tsp smoked paprika

pinch of dried chilli flakes

1 tsp rose harissa paste

1 tsp sunflower oil

1 large aubergine (eggplant), chopped into 2cm (¾in) chunks

12 button mushrooms

8 cherry tomatoes

pinch of smoked sea salt

Looking for something special to serve at your barbecue? Look no further than these simple kebabs. Aubergine, mushrooms and red onion are marinated in a smoky yogurt mix, before being grilled to tasty perfection. Serve with warmed pittas and a squeeze of lemon juice.

1 In a large bowl, whisk together the yogurt, smoked paprika, chilli flakes, rose harissa and sunflower oil. Season with smoked sea salt.

2 Stir in the aubergine, mushrooms and tomatoes and allow to marinate for 1 hour in a cool place.

3 Thread the aubergine, mushrooms and tomatoes onto skewers. Carefully place on a hot barbecue and cook for 3–4 minutes, turning frequently. Alternatively, heat a griddle (grill) pan and cook the skewers for 5–6 minutes, turning frequently.

EASY TIP
If you're using wooden skewers, be sure to soak them in water for at least 10 minutes before placing on the barbecue, or thread onto metal skewers.

Toasted almond, apricot and chickpea tagine

SERVES 4

2 tbsp sunflower oil

1 red onion, roughly chopped

2 carrots, peeled and roughly chopped

2 sweet potatoes, peeled and roughly chopped

¼ butternut squash, peeled, deseeded and roughly chopped

2 tsp ground cumin

1 tsp ground turmeric

2cm (¾in) piece of ginger, grated

2 garlic cloves, crushed

1 tsp rose harissa paste

juice of 2 unwaxed lemons

1 tbsp maple syrup

1 x 400g (14oz) can of chickpeas (garbanzo beans), drained and rinsed

generous handful of coriander (cilantro), roughly torn

15 dried apricots

2 tbsp toasted flaked (slivered) almonds

handful of flat-leaf parsley, finely chopped

Fragrant, bright and fresh, a great tagine is worth the wait. Cooking the tagine slowly allows the root vegetables to release their earthy, sweet flavours – and you don't even need a tagine dish! A simple lidded hob-to-oven pot works just as well.

1 Preheat the oven to 180°C/350°F/gas mark 4.

2 In a large, lidded flameproof dish, add the oil, red onion, carrots, sweet potatoes and butternut squash. Place over a medium-high heat and cook for 4–5 minutes, stirring frequently until the vegetables begin to soften. Stir in the cumin, turmeric, ginger and garlic and cook for a further 2 minutes until fragrant.

3 In a jug, mix together the harissa, lemon juice and maple syrup with 200ml (¾ cup) cold water. Pour this over the vegetable mix and stir through.

4 Stir in the chickpeas and coriander then top with the dried apricots. Place a lid on the dish and bake in the oven for 45–50 minutes until the vegetables are tender.

5 Remove from the oven and scatter with flaked almonds and flat-leaf parsley.

EASY TIP
Pre-toasted flaked almonds are available in supermarkets, or if you'd rather toast them yourself, simply add 2 tablespoons flaked almonds to a dry pan and toast for 3–4 minutes until light golden.

Carrot, orange and pistachio salad with za'atar and mint

SERVES 2

juice of ½ unwaxed orange

2 tbsp good-quality extra virgin olive oil

handful of coriander (cilantro), roughly chopped

½ tsp za'atar

6 large carrots, peeled and prepared in a combination of chopped, sliced into rounds or matchsticks and grated

handful of shelled pistachios, roughly chopped

drizzle of good-quality tahini

small handful of mint leaves, roughly torn

generous pinch each of sea salt and black pepper

Sometimes you're looking for a simple, elegant lunch. This salad has flavours of the Middle East, with fresh coriander and mint and freshly squeezed orange juice. Chop the carrots in various ways for interesting texture: grated, matchsticks and sliced into rounds; and if you can find tricolour carrots, these look beautiful served on a sharing platter.

1 In a jar, shake together the orange juice, olive oil, coriander, za'atar and sea salt until combined.

2 Pour the dressing over the carrots and stir through, along with the pistachios.

3 Drizzle over the tahini and scatter with the mint leaves. Season with black pepper.

EASY TIP

The dressing can be made up to 2 days in advance, but it is best to combine with the carrots just before serving so they remain crisp.

Potato latkes with deli pickle mayo

SERVES 4

2 large baking potatoes, peeled and coarsely grated

1 small red onion, coarsely grated

2 tsp plain (all-purpose) flour

pinch of smoked paprika

6 tbsp sunflower oil

4 tbsp vegan mayonnaise

small handful of dill, finely chopped

1 small pickled gherkin, finely chopped

1 tsp capers, drained

generous pinch of sea salt

Crisp on the outside and fluffy on the inside: who doesn't love a Jewish-style potato pancake? Generously spoon over cooling mayonnaise, inspired by the deli counter with flavours of dill, gherkins and capers. Simple, wholesome comfort food.

1 Place the grated potato and red onion on a clean, dry tea towel and squeeze out as much liquid as possible.

2 Add the drained potato and onion to a bowl and stir in the flour, smoked paprika and sea salt. Mix together until the grated potato is coated in the dry ingredients.

3 Heat the sunflower oil in a frying pan over a medium heat. Meanwhile, shape the potato mix into small, flat patties. Test that the oil is hot enough by adding in a couple of strands of grated potato – they should gently sizzle.

4 Carefully add the latkes to the pan and cook for 4–5 minutes on each side until golden. Do this in two batches if you need to, to avoid the latkes sticking together in the pan.

5 To make the deli pickle mayo, stir together the vegan mayonnaise, dill, chopped gherkin and capers.

6 Carefully remove the latkes from the pan and drain on kitchen paper. Spoon the deli pickle mayo over each of the latkes and serve hot.

EASY TIP
Vegan mayonnaise is readily available in supermarkets.

Herby no-meatballs

SERVES 4

3 tbsp sunflower oil

1 medium aubergine (eggplant), evenly diced

1 red onion, roughly chopped

1 tsp dried oregano

4 thick slices of white bread

handful of flat-leaf parsley, finely chopped

generous pinch each of sea salt and black pepper

This twist on a family-favourite is a little more elegant than processed vegan meatballs found in supermarkets. Aubergine delivers on the meaty texture, while red onion and herbs balance the flavours. Serve with tomato and chilli pasta sauce (page 309) and egg-free spaghetti, or loaded into a warmed baguette.

1 Heat 1 tablespoon of the oil in a large frying pan and add the aubergine, red onion and oregano. Cook over a medium-high heat for 10–12 minutes, stirring occasionally, until the aubergine has gently browned.

2 Add the bread to a food processor and blitz until you have fine breadcrumbs. Spoon into a bowl and set aside.

3 Add the cooked aubergine and red onion to the food processor and blitz until semi-smooth. Do not be tempted to add any water to the mix. Gradually add the breadcrumbs into the mix in three stages, blitzing after each stage, until it forms a firm mixture. Stir in the flat-leaf parsley and season generously with sea salt and black pepper. Allow the mixture to cool for a few minutes until you can comfortably handle it.

4 Heat the remaining 2 tablespoons oil in the frying pan over a medium-high heat. Roll half tablespoon-sized amounts of the mixture into even balls and carefully place in the oil. Cook for 3–4 minutes, then carefully turn the balls and cook for a further 3 minutes until golden on both sides.

EASY TIP

The no-meatball mixture can be made a day in advance.

MINUTE. 15 MINUTE.

Smoky aubergine, oregano and paprika stroganoff

SERVES 2

2 aubergines (eggplants), sliced lengthways into 5mm (¼in) thick slices

2 tbsp sunflower oil

¼ tsp dried oregano

1 small onion, diced

2 garlic cloves, crushed

250ml (1 cup) soya single (light) cream

1 tsp paprika

2 rounded tbsp plain soya yogurt

juice of ¼ unwaxed lemon

generous pinch each of sea salt and black pepper

Charred, herby aubergine slices and a creamy, subtly sour sauce offer a twist on a traditional stroganoff. Luxurious, unique and ready in just 15 minutes – what's not to love? Serve with fluffy rice, or over egg-free pasta.

1 Heat a large griddle (grill) pan over a high heat. Brush the aubergine slices over all surfaces with 1 tablespoon of the sunflower oil, then scatter over the oregano. Use tongs to place each slice on the griddle pan and cook for 3–4 minutes on each side until grill marks appear and the aubergine slices soften.

2 Meanwhile, heat the remaining tablespoon of oil in a large pan over a medium-high heat and throw in the onion. Cook for 2–3 minutes until softened, then add the garlic and cook for a further minute. Reduce the heat to medium, then pour in the soya cream and stir through the paprika. Simmer for 10 minutes, stirring occasionally.

3 Remove the creamy base from the heat and stir in the soya yogurt and lemon juice. Stir the hot, griddled aubergines into the sauce, then season to taste with salt and pepper. Serve hot.

EASY TIP

Use a plain, unsweetened soya yogurt to stir into the creamy paprika sauce for a taste of sour cream when combined with the lemon juice.

INGREDIENTS 5

Roasted fennel and butterbean gratin

SERVES 2

2 large fennel bulbs, sliced into even wedges

1 x 400g (14oz) can of butterbeans, drained and rinsed

200ml (generous ¾ cup) soya single (light) cream

1 garlic clove, peeled and crushed

pinch of grated nutmeg

generous pinch of sea salt

This simple dish started out life as a side dish in my house, but quickly became the star of the show as an elegant, fuss-free main meal. I love to serve with a rocket (arugula) salad, or with roasted broccoli with orange and almonds (page 294).

1 Preheat the oven to 200°C/400°F/gas mark 6.

2 Layer the sliced fennel and butterbeans into a baking dish, finishing with a layer of fennel.

3 Mix together the soya cream, garlic and nutmeg, then pour over the fennel and butterbeans. Bake in the oven for 20–22 minutes until the fennel is tender. Season to taste with sea salt.

EASY TIP
This recipe can be easily doubled up to serve more people.

Borlotti, blood orange and orzo with cinnamon

SERVES 4

1 tbsp sunflower oil

1 onion, thinly sliced

2 tsp rose harissa paste

pinch of dried chilli flakes

1 x 400g (14oz) can of good-quality chopped tomatoes

handful of cherry tomatoes

250g (1½ cups) dried orzo (ensure egg-free)

1 x 400g (14oz) can of borlotti beans, drained and rinsed

4 bay leaves

1 cinnamon stick

1 unwaxed blood orange, peeled and sliced into rounds (or use regular oranges if you can't get hold of blood variety)

juice of ½ unwaxed lemon

generous pinch each of sea salt and black pepper

A full-of-flavour dish that can be served in the oven dish – perfect for sharing on a celebratory evening. Drizzle over some tahini and pistachios, if you wish.

1 Preheat the oven to 180°C/350°F/gas mark 4.

2 In a large lidded flameproof casserole, heat the oil and onion over a medium-high heat for 5 minutes, stirring occasionally, until the onion begins to brown. Stir in the harissa and chilli flakes.

3 Pour in the chopped tomatoes then add the cherry tomatoes. Stir in the orzo with 250ml (1 cup) cold water, then pour the borlotti beans into the centre of the dish.

4 Push the bay leaves and cinnamon stick into the dish, then lay the orange slices over the top and place on the lid. Cook in the oven for 45 minutes, then increase the temperature to 200°C/400°F/gas mark 6 for 15 minutes.

5 Carefully remove from the oven and squeeze over the lemon juice. Season with salt and pepper.

EASY TIP

I love the nutty flavour of borlotti beans, but cannellini or butterbeans make good alternatives.

Cheat's spring risotto

SERVES 4

300g (1¼ cups) arborio rice

generous glug of white wine
(ensure vegan)

800ml (3⅓ cups) hot vegetable
stock

1 small leek, finely chopped

8 asparagus spears, tough ends
discarded

8 green beans, roughly
chopped

handful of frozen peas

4 leaves of spring greens,
roughly shredded

juice of ½ unwaxed lemon

generous handful of mint
leaves, finely chopped

small handful of flat-leaf parsley,
finely chopped

generous pinch each of sea salt
and black pepper

**Risotto can be tricky to make, especially when you're
cooking for guests. Spare yourself the worry by making
this cheat's version – which is cooked in the microwave!
This means a lot less stirring, and perfectly steamed
vegetables that remain *al dente*.**

1 Add the rice to a large, microwave-friendly bowl and
pour in the white wine. Stir in half of the stock and cover
with cling film (plastic wrap). Microwave for 10 minutes,
stir, then pour in the remaining stock and microwave for
a further 5 minutes.

2 Stir the rice and then add the leek, asparagus, green
beans, peas and spring greens. Re-cover the bowl then
microwave again for 5 minutes.

3 Remove from the microwave, stir and allow to stand
for a few moments. Stir through the lemon juice, mint
and parsley, then season to taste with salt and pepper.

EASY TIP
This recipe works best when cooked in a 850W
microwave.

Puy ragout

SERVES 4

Suitable for freezing

1 tbsp sunflower oil

1 onion, finely diced

1 carrot, peeled and sliced into rounds

1 celery stick, finely diced

8 button mushrooms, halved

2 garlic cloves, crushed

generous glug of red wine (ensure vegan)

1 tsp dried mixed herbs

1 tsp dried oregano

1 x 400g (14oz) can of chopped tomatoes

1 x 400g (14oz) can of Puy lentils, drained and rinsed

small handful of flat-leaf parsley, finely chopped

generous pinch each of sea salt and black pepper

Speed up a classic, slow-cooked ragout and have this French-inspired dish on the dinner table in just 30 minutes. Serve with mashed potatoes, creamy polenta, or stir it through pasta, if you like.

1 Heat the oil in a large pan over a medium-high heat and cook the onion, carrot, celery and mushrooms for 3 minutes until the vegetables begin to soften. Add the garlic and cook for a further minute.

2 Stir in the red wine, mixed herbs and oregano and reduce for 5 minutes.

3 Pour in the chopped tomatoes and lentils and cook for 20 minutes, stirring frequently to avoid sticking.

4 Season with sea salt and black pepper, then scatter with flat-leaf parsley just before serving.

EASY TIP

Puy lentils hold their shape better than green lentils, resulting in a meaty texture, especially alongside the mushrooms cooked in this ragout. French Puy lentils have a unique peppery flavour which adds to the depth of the dish.

Antipasti paella

SERVES 4

800ml (3⅓ cups) hot vegetable stock

generous glug of white wine (ensure vegan)

generous pinch of saffron strands

1 tbsp sunflower oil

1 onion, diced

2 garlic cloves, peeled and crushed

1 tsp smoked paprika

300g (1¼ cups) bomba rice (or use arborio)

handful of pitted black olives

12 semi-dried tomatoes

4 chargrilled (bell) peppers in oil, drained and roughly sliced

4 artichokes in oil, drained and roughly chopped

juice of 1 unwaxed lemon

handful of fresh flat-leaf parsley, finely chopped

generous pinch each of smoked sea salt and black pepper

lemon wedges, to serve

Paella is a real crowd-pleaser, especially in summer months when family and friends gather in the garden to enjoy some sunshine. Serve this sharing-style with a big spoon, so everyone can fill their bowl.

1 Mix the hot vegetable stock and white wine in a jug, then add the saffron. Stir and allow them to infuse the liquid.

2 Meanwhile, heat the oil in a large frying pan, add the onion and garlic and cook for 2–3 minutes over a medium heat, then stir in the smoked paprika.

3 Toss in the rice and coat in the cooked onion mix for 2 minutes. Stir in one-third of the saffron-infused vegetable stock. Cook for 10 minutes, stirring frequently, then add in another third of the stock, along with the olives, tomatoes, peppers and artichokes, and cook for a further 10 minutes.

4 Pour in the final third of the stock and cook for a further 8–10 minutes until the stock has been absorbed and the rice appears fluffy.

5 Remove the pan from the heat and stir through the lemon juice. Season with smoked sea salt and black pepper, then scatter with flat-leaf parsley and place the lemon wedges over the top.

EASY TIP

Good-quality saffron is an expensive ingredient, but it gives a golden colour to the rice and a subtle and unique 'honey' flavour to the dish. If you don't have saffron available, ¼ teaspon ground turmeric will deliver a vibrant colour.

POT · POT
1
POT · POT

Sweet potato, beer and lime chilli

SERVES 4

Suitable for freezing

2 medium-sized sweet potatoes, peeled and evenly diced into 2cm (¾in) chunks

1 yellow (bell) pepper, deseeded and roughly sliced

1 onion, finely diced

200ml (generous ¾ cup) dark beer (ensure vegan)

1 x 400g (14oz) can of chopped tomatoes

1 tbsp tomato ketchup

1 tsp mild chilli powder

1 tsp smoked paprika

1 tsp dried oregano

1 x 400g (14oz) can of kidney beans, drained and rinsed

150g (1 cup) canned or frozen sweetcorn

juice of 1 unwaxed lime

handful of coriander (cilantro), roughly torn

generous pinch each of smoked sea salt and black pepper

If you're looking to step up your veggie chilli game, look no further than this version, which is perfect for a relaxed Friday night feast. It's also suitable for freezing, making it the ideal dish for batch cooking. Serve with fresh tomato salsa (page 305) and paprika potato rounds (page 280) for an extra-special supper.

1 Add the diced sweet potato, pepper and onion to a large pan and pour over the beer. Bring to the boil over a medium heat for 10 minutes until the onion appears translucent.

2 Pour in the chopped tomatoes, ketchup, chilli powder, smoked paprika, oregano, kidney beans and sweetcorn, stir, then simmer for 30 minutes, stirring frequently to avoid sticking. Allow to reduce, then remove from the heat.

3 Stir in the lime juice and season to taste with salt and pepper. Scatter over the coriander just before serving.

EASY TIP

The variety of beer used gives varying flavours to this chilli. I love to use a dark beer, but a lighter IPA gives a subtler taste. Whichever beer you choose, ensure it is vegan-friendly.

Golden-battered tofish

SERVES 4

200g (generous 1½ cups) plain (all-purpose) flour

2 tbsp cornflour (cornstarch)

¼ tsp ground turmeric

small handful of dill, finely chopped

300ml (1¼ cups) chilled beer (ensure vegan)

2 x 280g (9oz) blocks of tofu, drained and pressed (see page 21)

4 sheets of sushi nori

500ml (2 cups) sunflower oil, for frying

1 tsp smoked sea salt, plus a generous pinch of black pepper

wedges of unwaxed lemon, to serve

Make every Friday a day to celebrate with this golden-battered tofish! Serve with chips, mint and lemon crushed peas (page 283) and tartare sauce (page 307).

1 In a large bowl, stir together the flour, cornflour, turmeric, dill, smoked salt and black pepper. Gradually pour in the beer and mix with a balloon whisk to get rid of any lumps. Rest the batter in the fridge for 15 minutes while you prepare the tofu.

2 Slice each block of pressed tofu horizontally so you have 4 slices, then press a sheet of nori on to each.

3 Heat the sunflower oil in a large, deep-sided frying pan over a medium heat. Check the oil is hot enough by dropping in a few drops of the batter; if it sizzles immediately it is ready. Dip the tofu slices in the batter to coat fully, then use a slotted spoon to place them in the pan for 4–5 minutes before turning and cooking the other side until light golden in colour.

4 Serve hot, with lemon wedges.

EASY TIP
Sushi nori sheets have a taste of the ocean. They can be found in large supermarkets, often stocked near ambient noodles and sushi rice.

Southern baked goujons

SERVES 4

8 rounded tbsp cornflakes (ensure vegan; see 'Easy Tip' below)

3 rounded tbsp vegan mayonnaise

drizzle of sunflower oil

generous pinch of smoked paprika

generous pinch of mild chilli powder

pinch of dried chilli flakes

280g (9oz) block of extra-firm tofu, drained and pressed (see page 21)

generous pinch each of sea salt and black pepper

Crisp, golden breadcrumbs give these tender goujons extra bite. Just a few store cupboard ingredients transform a simple block of tofu into this family favourite. Slice the tofu smaller to make baked nuggets instead, if you wish. Serve with ketchup.

1 Preheat the oven to 190°C/375°F/gas mark 5.

2 Spoon the cornflakes into a jug blender or food processor and blitz until a fine breadcrumb is created. Tip onto a plate and season with sea salt and plenty of black pepper.

3 In a bowl, stir together the vegan mayonnaise, sunflower oil, smoked paprika, chilli powder and chilli flakes until combined.

4 Slice the pressed tofu block horizontally into 3 slices, then cut each slice into 2cm (¾in) fingers. Dip each finger of tofu into the mayonnaise mix, then roll it into the cornflake breadcrumbs. Place on a baking tray and repeat with the remaining fingers of tofu.

5 Bake in the oven for 25 minutes until crisp. Serve hot.

EASY TIP

Some brands of cornflakes contain vitamin D from an animal source (often sheep's wool), making the product unsuitable for vegans. Many supermarket own brands do not fortify using this source of vitamin D, and do take a look at the cornflake brands in the free-from aisle of your local supermarket, as many of these will be labelled as vegan.

Charred mushroom steaks with chimichurri

SERVES 2

2 tbsp sunflower oil

2 tbsp light soy sauce

1 tbsp barbecue sauce (ensure vegan)

pinch of smoked paprika

2 large portobello mushrooms, stalks removed

For the chimichurri

handful of flat-leaf parsley

handful of coriander (cilantro)

½ small red onion, roughly chopped

1 garlic clove, peeled

pinch of dried chilli flakes

200ml (generous ¾ cup) good-quality extra virgin olive oil

2 tbsp apple cider vinegar

generous pinch of sea salt

Smoky, meaty and 100 per cent vegan, these charred mushroom steaks are the perfect treat for two. I love to cook them on a hot griddle (grill) pan, but they also cook well on an electric grilling machine. Serve with chunky chips, or in toasted ciabatta as a charred mushroom steak sandwich.

1 Heat a griddle pan over a medium-high heat until hot.

2 In a bowl, whisk together the sunflower oil, soy sauce, barbecue sauce and smoked paprika. Brush the mix generously onto all surfaces of the mushrooms.

3 Carefully place the mushrooms on the hot griddle pan and cook for 4–5 minutes on each side, pressing down lightly with tongs to create grill lines.

4 Meanwhile, put the parsley, coriander, onion, garlic, chilli flakes and olive oil into a high-powered blender and blitz until semi-smooth. Stir in the cider vinegar and season to taste with sea salt.

5 Drizzle the chimichurri generously over the charred mushroom steaks just before serving.

EASY TIP

Both the marinade and the chimichurri can be made up to 2 days in advance when kept in the fridge.

Carvery-filled Yorkshire puddings

MAKES ABOUT 8

Suitable for freezing

For the Yorkshire puddings

200g (generous 1½ cups) plain (all-purpose) flour, sifted

½ tsp baking powder

pinch of fine sea salt

400ml (generous 1½ cups) soya milk, chilled

8 tsp sunflower oil

For the carvery filling

1 tbsp sunflower oil

pinch of dried sage

¼ red cabbage, shredded

¼ onion, sliced

1 carrot, peeled and thinly sliced

4 small florets of Tenderstem broccoli, sliced in half

handful of pecans, roughly chopped

handful of frozen peas

When you think a vegan Yorkshire pudding can't get any better, load it with sage, vegetables and pecans. Perfect for Sunday dinner (and for any other dinner!), serve with lashings of onion and thyme gravy (page 309).

1 Preheat the oven to 220°C/425°F/gas mark 7.

2 In a large jug, stir together the flour, baking powder and salt. Pour in the soya milk and lightly whisk until smooth.

3 Spoon 1 teaspoon of oil into each hole of an 8-hole muffin tin, and place in the oven for 5–7 minutes until the oil is very hot.

4 Carefully remove the hot muffin tin from the oven and pour in the batter, to fill half of each hole. Cook in the oven for 25 minutes until golden and risen.

5 Meanwhile, prepare the filling. Heat the oil in a wok and throw in the sage, red cabbage, onion, carrot, broccoli and pecans, then stir-fry over a high heat for 4–5 minutes. Add the peas and cook for a further minute.

6 Turn off the oven and allow the Yorkshire puddings to stand for a further 5 minutes. Then open the oven door slightly and allow to stand for another 5 minutes (this will ensure that the Yorkshire puddings stay risen until they reach your plate).

7 Load the filling into the Yorkshire puddings, and serve hot with gravy.

EASY TIP

If time allows, refrigerate the batter for 1 hour, but if you need these Yorkshire puddings in a hurry, ensure the soya milk is chilled before use.

Stovetop haggis

SERVES 4

Suitable for freezing

1 tbsp sunflower oil

1 onion, diced

2 carrots, peeled and diced

1 tsp ground cinnamon

1 tsp dried mixed herbs

1 tsp dried sage

4 tbsp pearl barley

3 tbsp dried red lentils

2 tsp rolled oats

1 x 400g (14oz) can of green lentils, drained and rinsed

500ml (2 cups) hot vegetable stock

1 tsp yeast extract

generous pinch each of sea salt and black pepper

For Burns night and beyond! This vegan twist on the Scottish classic of haggis is warming, comforting and gives a sense of occasion to any winter celebration. There's no need to bake this haggis in the oven, it becomes perfectly cooked on the hob. Serve with neeps and tatties (of course!).

1 Heat the oil in a large pan or flameproof casserole dish, add the onion and cook over a medium heat for 4–5 minutes until it becomes golden. Add the carrots, cinnamon, mixed herbs and sage and cook for a further minute.

2 Spoon in the pearl barley, red lentils, rolled oats and green lentils, then pour in the hot vegetable stock. Cook for 20 minutes without covering with a lid, stirring frequently over a medium-high heat, then reduce the heat and simmer for another 20 minutes. Don't be tempted to add more liquid, the haggis should be stodgy, and most of the liquid should be absorbed or evaporated.

3 Spoon in the yeast extract and stir through. Cook for a further 5 minutes. Remove from the heat and season to taste with sea salt and plenty of black pepper.

EASY TIP

The quantities are easy to double up if you're serving more guests.

Chestnut and cranberry rolls

SERVES 2

---

1 tbsp sunflower oil, plus 2 tsp
for brushing

1 small onion, diced

1 tsp dried sage

180g (1 cup) vacuum-packed
roasted chestnuts, finely
chopped

4 sheets of filo pastry (ensure
dairy-free)

4 tsp cranberry sauce

generous pinch each of sea salt
and black pepper

**One bite of these festive rolls, and you'll step right
into the holiday season! Serve either hot or cold, as an
alternative to vegan sausage rolls, with a small bowl of
five-spice cranberry sauce (page 310) for dipping.**

1 Preheat the oven to 200°C/400°F/gas mark 6 and
line two baking trays with baking parchment.

2 Heat the 1 tablespoon sunflower oil in a large pan,
then add the onion and dried sage. Cook for 2–3 minutes,
stirring frequently, until the onion starts to soften.

3 Add the chopped chestnuts then cook for another
2 minutes. Season with sea salt and black pepper, then
remove from the heat.

4 Lay out one sheet of the filo pastry on a clean, flat
surface. Use a pastry brush to sweep over a little
sunflower oil, and place over a second sheet of filo pastry.

5 Spoon 2 teaspoons cranberry sauce in a straight line
4cm (1½in) from the top of the pastry. Spoon half of the
chestnut mixture over the cranberry sauce. Roll the pastry
to form a log shape, tightly to secure the filling.

6 Use a sharp knife to cut the roll into 6 even pieces,
then place on a baking tray. Brush the tops with a little
sunflower oil. Repeat with the remaining 2 pastry sheets,
cranberry sauce and chestnut filling.

7 Bake in the oven for 25 minutes until golden and crisp.

EASY TIP

Use the pastry sheets straight from the pack, as they
will dry out quickly if left without moisture from the
other sheets, or cover with a clean, damp cloth.

Creamy mushroom and thyme canapés

MAKES ABOUT 10

1 sheet of ready-rolled puff pastry (ensure dairy-free), at room temperature

2 tsp soya milk, to glaze

1 tbsp sunflower oil

10 button mushrooms, halved

1 sprig of fresh thyme, leaves finely chopped

5 tbsp soya single (light) cream

generous pinch each of sea salt and black pepper

Perfect for parties and picnics alike, these bite-sized treats are easy to eat and delicious. Feel free to add some fresh garlic when you cook the mushrooms and thyme, or scatter with flat-leaf parsley before serving, but I enjoy the simplicity of these canapés, especially served with a chilled aperitif.

1 Preheat the oven to 220°C/425°F/gas mark 7 and line a baking tray with baking parchment.

2 Lay the puff pastry sheet on a flat surface and use a round 5cm (2in) cutter to press out pastry circles. Place them on the baking tray. Using a smaller 4cm (1½in) cutter, press gently into the centre of each pastry disc to leave a light indentation – this shouldn't cut through the pastry. Lay each round on the lined baking tray and brush the outer area with a soya milk. Bake in the oven for 10–12 minutes until risen and golden.

3 Meanwhile, heat the oil in a frying pan and fry the mushrooms and thyme for 4–5 minutes until softened and fragrant. Spoon in the soya cream and stir. Season to taste with sea salt and plenty of black pepper.

4 Carefully remove the baking tray from the oven. Push down the centres of the pastry cups, then spoon teaspoon-sized amounts of the creamy mushrooms into each. Serve warm or at room temperature.

EASY TIP

To avoid the pastry going soggy, it's best to assemble the canapés just before serving. The pastry cups and the creamy mushrooms can both be made up to a day in advance.

Chestnut cassoulet

SERVES 4

Suitable for freezing

1 tbsp sunflower oil

1 onion, finely diced

2 celery sticks, diced

2 carrots, peeled and sliced into half-rounds

2 large leaves of cavolo nero, shredded

2 garlic cloves, crushed

½ tsp dried sage

generous glug of red wine (ensure vegan)

1 x 400g (14oz) can of good-quality chopped tomatoes

300ml (1¼ cups) hot vegetable stock

200g (1¼ cups) vacuum-packed roasted chestnuts

1 sprig of fresh rosemary

1 sprig of fresh thyme

zest of 1 unwaxed orange

generous pinch each of sea salt and black pepper

Nothing says Christmas like chestnuts, sage and orange, cooked into a classic cassoulet with red wine. Elegant, delicious and perfect for festive celebrations served alongside fail-safe roast potatoes (page 291) and root gratin (page 289). It's also cooked on the hob in just one pot, meaning less fuss and washing up!

1 Heat the oil in a large pan, add the onion and cook over a medium heat for 2–3 minutes until the onion starts to soften. Add the celery, carrots and cavolo nero and cook for a further 2 minutes.

2 Throw in the garlic and dried sage and cook for 1 minute until the garlic becomes fragrant, then pour in the red wine and reduce for 2–3 minutes.

3 Stir in the chopped tomatoes, stock and chestnuts, then add the rosemary and thyme and simmer for 30–35 minutes, stirring occasionally to avoid sticking, until the cassoulet has reduced slightly.

4 Remove from the heat and stir in the orange zest. Season to taste with salt and pepper.

EASY TIP

Vacuum-packed roasted chestnuts can be found in most supermarkets, making them a convenient and speedy way to cook with chestnuts. If you'd prefer to roast fresh chestnuts at home, simply use a sharp knife to cut a cross into the skin of each nut, then roast in the oven for 30–35 minutes at 200°C/400°F/gas mark 6. Allow to cool before peeling away the skin and white pith.

Boxing Day curry

SERVES 4

Suitable for freezing

1 tbsp sunflower oil

1 onion, finely diced

2 garlic cloves, crushed

1 tsp ground cumin

1 tsp ground turmeric

generous pinch of dried chilli flakes

2 rounded tbsp medium curry paste (ensure dairy-free)

2 x 400g (14oz) cans of full-fat coconut milk

1 tbsp cranberry sauce

a selection of leftover roasted vegetables, including carrots, parsnips, red onions, sprouts, butternut squash, chopped into bite-sized chunks

2 handfuls of raisin and nut mix, roughly chopped

juice of ½ unwaxed lemon

generous handful of coriander (cilantro), roughly torn

generous pinch of sea salt

Use up those leftover roasted vegetables, raisins, nuts and cranberry sauce in this warming and creamy curry – that conveniently takes just 15 minutes to make (because who wants to be cooking for longer than this on Boxing Day?). Serve with easy pilau rice (page 300) as a seasonal, cinnamon-infused side dish.

1 In a large pan, heat the oil and onion over a high heat for 2–3 minutes until the onion begins to soften. Add the garlic, cumin, turmeric and chilli flakes and cook for 1 minute.

2 Add the curry paste, coconut milk and cranberry sauce, then bring to the boil and simmer for 10 minutes, stirring occasionally, until the coconut milk has thickened slightly.

3 Spoon in the leftover roasted vegetables, raisins and nuts and heat through for 1 minute. Remove from the heat and stir in the lemon juice. Season to taste with sea salt and scatter with coriander just before serving.

EASY TIP

If you don't have any leftover roasted vegetables, simply place carrots, parsnips, red onion, sprouts and butternut squash on a baking tray with a drizzle of sunflower oil and roast at 200°C/400°F/gas mark 6 for 35–40 minutes, turning once.

Sweet

Chai roasted rhubarb crumble

SERVES 4

400g (14oz) rhubarb, sliced into 4cm (1½in) pieces

2 tbsp caster (superfine) sugar

juice of ½ unwaxed orange

¼ tsp ground cinnamon

¼ tsp grated nutmeg

¼ ground allspice

For the crumble topping

100g (scant 1 cup) plain (all-purpose) flour

50g (¼ cup) demerara sugar

50g (½ cup) rolled oats

2 tbsp vegan butter, at room temperature

2 tbsp shelled pistachios, roughly chopped

Pink and tender roasted rhubarb takes on the flavours of orange and chai spices before being topped with a nutty crumble. Pudding doesn't get much better than this! Serve with vanilla custard (page 272).

1 Preheat the oven to 200°C/400°F/gas mark 6.

2 Lay the sliced rhubarb in a single layer in a large ovenproof dish and scatter with the sugar. Squeeze in the orange juice and sprinkle with cinnamon, nutmeg and allspice. Cover loosely with foil and cook in the oven for 15–20 minutes until softened.

3 Meanwhile, stir together the flour, sugar and oats in a bowl. Rub in the vegan butter until the mixture resembles breadcrumbs. Stir in the chopped pistachios. Spoon onto a baking tray, then bake in the oven for 8–10 minutes until golden and toasted.

4 Remove the cooked fruit and crumble topping from the oven. Spoon the topping over the fruit just before serving.

EASY TIP
Cooking the fruit in a separate baking dish to the topping, then assembling just before serving keeps the topping crisp and delicious.

Lemon and rosemary rice pudding

SERVES 2 GENEROUSLY

100g (generous ½ cup) pudding rice

800ml (3⅓ cups) vanilla flavoured soya milk

1 rounded tbsp caster (superfine) sugar

1 sprig of fresh rosemary

zest and juice of 1 unwaxed lemon

Rice pudding is comfort food royalty, and this version has a rosemary-infused flavour with fresh lemon zest and juice. I've even been known to enjoy this pudding chilled, as a summery alternative to the traditional hot dessert. Pudding rice is available in supermarkets, and is flaked for a shorter cooking time.

1 Tip the rice into a large pan and stir in the soya milk and sugar. Bring to a simmer over a medium heat, then add the sprig of rosemary. Simmer for 5 minutes, stirring frequently.

2 Stir in the lemon zest and juice and cook for a further 5–6 minutes until the rice pudding has thickened.

3 Remove and discard the rosemary sprig and serve in warmed bowls.

EASY TIP

Vanilla flavoured soya milk can be found in large supermarkets and health food stores. It's sweet, creamy and contrasts perfectly with the lemon zest. If you don't have any available, use sweetened soya milk and stir in a teaspoon of good-quality vanilla paste.

Upside-down mini cheesecakes

SERVES 4

4 tsp strawberry jam

4 strawberries, sliced

200g (scant 1 cup) mild vegan cream cheese

zest of 1 unwaxed lemon

3 ginger biscuits (ensure dairy-free), blitzed to a fine crumb in a food processor or broken with a rolling pin

Cheesecake in an instant! These fun desserts have a sweet fruity layer at the bottom and a creamy, lemony centre before being topped with ginger biscuit crumbs.

1 Spoon the jam into four ramekins and spread it out over the base of the dish. Lay over the strawberry slices.

2 In a bowl, stir together the vegan cream cheese and lemon zest. Mix until smooth. Spoon into the ramekins over the strawberry slices.

3 Generously sprinkle over the biscuit crumb, and chill in the fridge until ready to eat.

EASY TIP

Use a mild vegan cream cheese in this recipe, avoiding any that are labelled 'mature', 'cheddar-style' or with any additional flavours such as chives. You'll find mild vegan cream cheese in most large supermarkets.

Rum and raisin barbecue bananas

SERVES 4

4 tbsp raisins

2 tbsp dark rum

1 rounded tbsp vegan butter

2 tsp black treacle

4 bananas, unpeeled, sliced with a knife lengthways to make a pocket (but don't cut all the way through)

Is it even a barbecue without a baked banana? These boozy, buttery baked bananas have a kick of dark rum, black treacle and infused raisins – a perfect treat for the adults.

1 Add the raisins to a small bowl, then pour over the rum. Allow to stand for 15 minutes until the raisins have absorbed the rum.

2 Spoon in the vegan butter and black treacle and stir until everything is combined in the butter.

3 Lay each banana on a separate piece of foil, big enough to fold around it. Add a few teaspoons of the rum and raisin butter mix to each banana, then wrap in the foil.

4 Place on the barbecue (grill) for 12–15 minutes until the bananas have softened and caramelized.

EASY TIP

These bananas can be prepared a few hours in advance, and then cooked to order on the barbecue!

Limoncello panna cotta

SERVES 4

1 x 400ml (14fl oz) can of full-fat coconut milk

2 tbsp caster (superfine) sugar

2 tsp agar agar flakes

2 tbsp good-quality limoncello

zest of 1 unwaxed lemon

Simple, refreshing and perfectly balanced, this dessert is the ideal option to follow a heavy meal. For an unexpected flavour twist, throw a sprig of fresh thyme into the pan; simply discard before pouring the mixture into dariole moulds.

1 Add the coconut milk, sugar, agar agar flakes and limoncello to a pan and bring to a simmer over a medium heat for 5 minutes until you can see that all of the agar agar flakes have fully dissolved. Stir in the lemon zest.

2 Pour the mixture into four small dariole moulds, then chill in the fridge overnight, or for at least 6 hours, to allow the mixture to set.

3 Remove the panna cotta from the fridge and place the containers in a bowl of hot water for up to a minute, to make removal easier. Place the dariole moulds on serving plates and gently shake to allow the panna cotta to slide onto the plates. Serve immediately.

EASY TIP

Agar agar flakes are available in the baking aisle of large supermarkets, and also in Chinese supermarkets.

Baked apricots with marzipan and rosemary

SERVES 4

juice of 1 unwaxed orange

1 sprig of rosemary

8 ripe apricots, halved and stoned

100g (3½oz) marzipan (ensure egg-free), cut into pieces

2 tsp flaked (slivered) almonds

Warm apricots are magical, especially when filled with marzipan and toasted almonds and oven-poached in orange juice and rosemary. Serve with vegan vanilla ice cream.

1 Preheat the oven to 180°C/350°F/gas mark 4.

2 Squeeze the orange juice into a deep roasting tray and add the rosemary sprig.

3 Arrange the apricot halves cut side up in the roasting tray, and fill each half with pieces of marzipan.

4 Bake in the oven for 20 minutes, then carefully scatter with flaked almonds and return to the oven for a further 15 minutes until the apricots are tender and the almonds look toasted.

EASY TIP

You can find marzipan available in most supermarkets, in the baking supplies aisle. Choose from golden marzipan or white, but do check the ingredients as some brands may contain egg.

Easy chocolate cupcakes

MAKES ABOUT 12

Suitable for freezing

240ml (1 cup) sweetened soya milk

1 tsp apple cider vinegar

150g (¾ cup) granulated sugar

100ml (scant ½ cup) sunflower oil

1 tsp good-quality vanilla extract

150g (1¼ cups) plain (all-purpose) flour

50g (½ cup) cocoa powder

¾ tsp bicarbonate of soda (baking soda)

½ tsp baking powder

This is a recipe I've used for many years, and it never fails to produce light, well-risen cupcakes that are full of flavour. Use this recipe as a base to add in additional flavours such as orange or mint extract. Top with fail-safe buttercream (opposite).

1 Preheat the oven to 190°C/375°F/gas mark 5 and line a 12-hole cupcake tray with paper cases.

2 In a jug, whisk together the soya milk and cider vinegar. Leave to stand for a couple of minutes until it appears thickened. Whisk in the sugar, sunflower oil and vanilla extract.

3 In a large bowl, stir together the flour, cocoa powder, bicarbonate of soda and baking powder. Pour in the liquid mixture from the jug and fold until just combined.

4 Spoon the cake batter evenly into the paper cases. Bake in the oven for 18–20 minutes until springy to the touch and slightly shiny on the top.

5 Allow to cool fully before icing with buttercream.

EASY TIP
Whisking a teaspoon of cider vinegar into soya milk creates a rich buttermilk, which will give a luxurious texture to the cupcakes, without the use of dairy.

MINUTE. MINUTE. 15

Fail-safe buttercream

ENOUGH FOR
12 CUPCAKES, OR
1 LARGER SANDWICH CAKE

200g (scant 1 cup) vegan butter,
at room temperature

450g (3½ cups) icing
(confectioners') sugar

1 tsp good-quality vanilla
extract

2 tsp sweetened soya milk
(see 'Easy Tip' below)

Every home baker needs a fail-safe vegan buttercream recipe, for frosting, spreading, piping and cake decorating. This basic recipe works as a base for extra flavourings and vegan-friendly food colourings. Vegan butter varies in oil content across brands, so you may find that you don't need to add in the soya milk if the vegan butter you're using has a higher proportion of oil.

1 In a large bowl, use a fork to beat the vegan butter until softened.

2 Sift in half of the icing sugar and mix with a wooden spoon until combined. Sift in the remaining half and fold to form a stiff mixture.

3 Spoon in the vanilla extract and soya milk, then use an electric whisk to beat for 4–5 minutes until light and paler in colour.

EASY TIP

If you're using the buttercream to pipe onto cupcakes, keep the mixture stiff without adding soya milk. If you're using it to spread smoothly onto a cake, soya milk will give it a lighter consistency.

Lemon drizzle squares

MAKES ABOUT 8

*Suitable for freezing
(without the drizzle)*

250g (2 cups) self-raising flour

100g (½ cup) caster (superfine) sugar

¾ tsp baking powder

250ml (1 cup) sweetened soya milk

100ml (scant ½ cup) sunflower oil

1 tsp good-quality vanilla extract

zest and juice of ½ unwaxed lemon

For the drizzle

zest and juice of ½ unwaxed lemon

150g (1¼ cups) icing (confectioners') sugar, sifted

Light, zesty and made for sharing, these lemon drizzle squares will delight everyone who is lucky enough to try one! Mix up the flavours seasonally – try with unwaxed lime or orange.

1 Preheat the oven to 180°C/350°F/gas mark 4. Line a small baking tray (30x20cm/12x8in) with baking parchment.

2 In a large bowl, stir together the flour, sugar and baking powder. In a jug, whisk together the soya milk, sunflower oil, vanilla extract, lemon zest and juice. Fold the liquid mixture into the dry ingredients until just combined.

3 Pour into the lined baking tray, then bake in the oven for 20–25 minutes until lightly golden and risen.

4 Meanwhile, prepare the drizzle. Mix together the lemon zest, juice and icing sugar in a small bowl until smooth. Set aside at room temperature.

5 Remove the lemon cake from the oven and allow to cool in the tin for a few minutes. Drizzle over the icing, then slice into even squares.

EASY TIP
These cake squares will keep for up to 3 days when stored in a sealed container, in a cool, dry place.

Bakewell tart flapjack

MAKES 8 SQUARES

4 tbsp sunflower oil

4 rounded tbsp golden syrup

½ tsp good-quality almond extract

200g (2 cups) rolled oats

2 rounded tbsp flaked (slivered) almonds, plus extra for topping

1 tbsp glacé cherries, roughly chopped

2 tbsp cherry jam

Combine two British classic bakes into this ultimate vegan hybrid flapjack. Perfect for lunchboxes, it will keep for up to 4 days when stored in a sealed container.

1 Preheat the oven to 200°C/400°F/gas mark 6 and line a small baking tray (30x20cm/12x8in) with baking parchment.

2 In a large bowl, stir together the oil, syrup and almond extract until combined.

3 Stir in the oats, almonds and glacé cherries and mix until coated in the syrup mixture.

4 Press half of the mixture into the baking tray, smoothing it with a spatula. Spoon over the cherry jam and distribute evenly. Press the remaining half of the oat mix over the jam and smooth with a spatula.

5 Bake in the oven for 15 minutes, then carefully remove the tray from the oven. Press on the extra flaked almonds using the back of a spoon, then return to the oven for 5 minutes until the almonds appear lightly toasted.

6 Remove from the oven and allow to cool before slicing into squares.

EASY TIP

Don't worry if the flapjacks don't appear 'set' when first removed from the oven, they will become firmer and chewier as they cool down.

Sticky ginger parkin

SERVES 8

Suitable for freezing

150g (1¼ cups) plain (all-purpose) flour

1 tsp baking powder

½ tsp bicarbonate of soda (baking soda)

3 tsp ground ginger

1 tsp grated nutmeg

1 tsp mixed spice

1 tsp ground cinnamon

50ml (scant ¼ cup) soya milk

120ml (½ cup) sunflower oil

2 rounded tbsp black treacle

2 rounded tbsp golden syrup

2 tbsp vanilla soya yogurt

These sticky squares of cake are flavoured with black treacle, golden syrup and warming spices. I love serving this parkin warm on Bonfire Night, for a sweet treat that everyone will love. Perfect for autumn through to winter.

1 Preheat the oven to 180°C/350°F/gas mark 4 and line a 23cm (9in) square baking tin with baking parchment.

2 Mix the flour, baking powder, bicarbonate of soda, ginger, nutmeg, mixed spice and cinnamon in a bowl.

3 In a separate bowl, whisk together the soya milk, sunflower oil, black treacle, golden syrup and soya yogurt until combined. Pour the dry ingredients into the wet mixture and stir together until just combined.

4 Pour into the lined tin and bake in the oven for 25–30 minutes. Allow to cool before slicing into 8 pieces.

EASY TIP
Adding yogurt to the sponge mix ensures a moist, fudgy texture.

Clementine curd

MAKES 1 SMALL JAR

zest and juice of 3 unwaxed
clementines

150g (¾ cup) granulated sugar

400ml (generous 1½ cups)
sweetened soya milk

1 tbsp cornflour (cornstarch)

1 tbsp vegan butter

**A jar of clementine curd is a well-appreciated holiday
season gift, or if you'd rather keep it all to yourself
(who can blame you), smooth it over hot crumpets or
chocolate cake as an alternative to buttercream.**

1 Add the clementine zest and juice, sugar, soya milk and
cornflour to a pan, then bring to a simmer for 10 minutes
over a medium heat. Whisk frequently until it begins to
thicken.

2 Stir in the vegan butter and cook for a further 2 minutes
until smooth.

3 Allow to cool a little, then pour into a clean jar.
Refrigerate overnight until set.

EASY TIP
This curd will last up to one week in a clean, sealed jar in
the fridge.

Blackberry and mint coulis

SERVES 4

Suitable for freezing

250g (2½ cups) fresh blackberries

2 tbsp caster (superfine) sugar

½ tsp good-quality vanilla extract

small handful of fresh mint leaves, roughly torn

This versatile sauce is easy to prepare with a few simple ingredients, in under 15 minutes. Drizzle over ice cream, pancakes or creamy coconut yogurt.

1 Put the blackberries and sugar into a pan and pour in 150ml (generous ½ cup) cold water.

2 Bring to the boil over a low-medium heat and cook for 6–8 minutes, stirring frequently, until the fruit becomes soft and jammy. Use a wooden spoon to break up the fruit as it cooks.

3 Stir in the vanilla extract and mint leaves and cook for a further minute.

4 Transfer to a high-powered jug blender and blitz until smooth. Push through a sieve, using a spoon, for the smoothest coulis.

EASY TIP
Use this as a base recipe for other soft fruit coulis combinations, including blueberry and cinnamon or strawberry and lime.

Salted caramel sauce

MAKES 1 JAR

Suitable for freezing

3 tbsp soft light brown sugar

2 rounded tbsp golden syrup

1 rounded tbsp vegan butter

1 tsp good-quality vanilla extract

½ tsp sea salt, plus extra for sprinkling

250ml (1 cup) soya single (light) cream

Who doesn't love a silky, salted caramel sauce? A sprinkle of sea salt enhances the sweet notes in the sauce, while balancing the flavours for a crowd-pleasing favourite. Pour this over pecan and nutmeg banana loaf (page 250), baked apples, or ice cream.

1 Melt the sugar, syrup, vegan butter, vanilla extract and sea salt in a pan over a low heat for 5–6 minutes without stirring, until it bubbles.

2 Remove from the heat and allow to cool for a few minutes. Whisk in the soya cream until combined and smooth. Sprinkle with a little extra sea salt just before serving.

EASY TIP

Use good-quality sea salt flakes for the best flavour contrast in this sauce.

Peanut butter cup spread

MAKES 1 SMALL JAR

100g (3½oz) dark chocolate (ensure dairy-free)

3 tbsp soya single (light) cream

1 tbsp maple syrup

200g (7oz) smooth peanut butter, at room temperature

pinch of sea salt

Get that all-American hit of chocolate and peanut butter, simply by using store cupboard ingredients! This spread is delicious smoothed on toasted crumpets, or as a dip for sliced apples.

1 Break the chocolate into even pieces, and place in a heatproof bowl. Bring a pan of water to a gentle simmer over a low-medium heat and place the bowl over the pan, ensuring that the base is not directly touching the water. Stir the chocolate occasionally to distribute the heat, then, when the chocolate has melted, carefully remove the bowl from the pan and whisk in the soya cream and maple syrup.

2 Spoon the peanut butter into the bowl of melted chocolate, along with a pinch of salt. Stir and mix until fully combined. Spoon into a clean jar, allow to cool until set, then store in the fridge.

EASY TIP

The oil content in peanut butter varies between brands, so if it's proving difficult to combine the chocolate and peanut butter together, mix in a tablespoon of melted coconut oil.

Gingerbread pancakes

MAKES ABOUT 6

100g (scant 1 cup) plain (all-purpose) flour

½ tsp ground ginger

½ tsp ground cinnamon

pinch of grated nutmeg

200ml (generous ¾ cup) sweetened soya milk, chilled

6 tbsp sunflower oil,

For warming winter treats and beyond! These classic pancakes have the distinctive taste of gingerbread – with very little effort on your behalf. Serve with a generous drizzle of maple syrup and a sprinkle of unwaxed lemon zest, to make the gingerbread flavour pop!

1 In a large bowl, stir together the flour, ginger, cinnamon and nutmeg until combined. Pour in the soya milk and whisk to create a smooth batter. Chill in the fridge for 1 hour.

2 Add a tablespoon of sunflower oil to a pancake pan over a medium-high heat. Test if the oil is hot by dripping a small amount of the chilled mixture into the pan; if it sizzles and becomes golden within 20 seconds, it is hot enough. Swirl in 4 tablespoons of the batter and cook for 2–3 minutes, then flip the pancake over and cook the other side.

3 Drain on kitchen paper and keep warm while you repeat the process, using 1 tablespoon of sunflower oil per pancake.

EASY TIP

Chilling the pancake batter for an hour before making the pancakes gives the best texture, or use chilled soya milk if you simply don't have the time to wait.

Pecan and nutmeg banana loaf

MAKES 1 LOAF

Suitable for freezing

3 very ripe bananas, peeled

25g (2 tbsp) granulated sugar

25g (2 tbsp) soft light brown sugar

80ml (⅓ cup) sunflower oil

230g (scant 2 cups) self-raising flour

1 tsp bicarbonate of soda (baking soda)

1 tsp grated nutmeg

pinch of ground cinnamon

50g (scant ½ cup) pecans, roughly chopped

pinch of salt

This all-in-one loaf recipe bakes a fluffy banana cake, flavoured with nutmeg, cinnamon and pecans, and has a moreish crust. Perfect for lunchboxes and great for using up those overripe bananas!

1 Preheat the oven to 180°C/350°F/gas mark 4. Line a 450g (1lb) loaf tin with baking parchment.

2 Mash the bananas vigorously with a fork to create a smooth mixture. Stir in the granulated sugar, brown sugar and sunflower oil.

3 Sift in the flour, bicarbonate of soda, nutmeg, cinnamon, pecans and salt and stir to form a batter.

4 Pour into the lined loaf tin, then bake in the oven for 50–55 minutes until risen and the top is golden brown. Allow to cool slightly before slicing.

EASY TIP

For best results, use very ripe bananas with brown speckled peels.

Mocha mug brownie

SERVES 1

2 tbsp self-raising flour

2 tbsp cocoa powder

2 tbsp caster (superfine) sugar

2 tsp good-quality instant coffee

1 tbsp sunflower oil

drizzle of soya single (light) cream, to serve

For when you need a warm, chocolate brownie, with a hint of coffee in under 5 minutes. You're welcome.

1 In a large mug, mix together the flour, cocoa powder, sugar and coffee.

2 Pour in the sunflower oil with 4 tablespoons boiling water and whisk with a fork until combined into a batter.

3 Cook in a 800W microwave for 2 minutes, then allow to stand for 1 minute before drizzling with a little soya cream.

EASY TIP

Allow the brownie to cool for a few minutes before enjoying, as it will be *very* hot.

Berry crumble in a mug

SERVES 1

3 rounded tbsp frozen red berries

2 tsp caster (superfine) sugar

juice of 1 unwaxed lemon

1 tbsp soft light brown sugar

1 vegan digestive biscuit (graham cracker), crushed into rough crumbs

1 tsp rolled oats

1 rounded tsp vegan butter

Satisfy those sweet cravings with a quick berry crumble, made in a mug. I love the flavours of mixed red berries in this crumble, and I always have some in the freezer for crumble emergencies. Serve topped with a spoonful of thick coconut yogurt.

1 Spoon the frozen berries, caster sugar and lemon juice into a large, microwave-safe mug. Cover with cling film (plastic wrap) and pierce the top. Cook in a 800W microwave for 1 minute 30 seconds, then remove and stir. Drain away any excess liquid.

2 In a small bowl, combine the brown sugar, crushed digestive biscuit and oats. Rub in the vegan butter to create a crumbly texture.

3 Spoon the topping over the cooked fruit, then cook again in microwave for 1 minute. Allow to cool for a few minutes before enjoying.

EASY TIP

If you don't have dairy-free digestive biscuits available, dairy-free ginger biscuits or oat biscuits are also delicious in this crumble topping.

Berry bruschetta

SERVES 4

8 strawberries, sliced

8 raspberries, halved

8 blackberries, halved

generous handful of
blueberries

juice of ¼ unwaxed lemon

4 thick slices of white baguette
(French stick)

4 tsp vanilla soya yogurt

drizzle of maple syrup

**This is a great recipe to make when you have lots of
berries to use up. It's also a balanced and delicious
dessert for children (and adults too!).**

1 Add the berries to a bowl and squeeze over the lemon
juice. Stir through and allow to stand while you prepare
the toasts.

2 Heat a griddle (grill) pan over a medium-high heat,
then add the baguette slices. Toast for 2–3 minutes on
each side, until grill lines appear.

3 Remove from the griddle pan and smooth over
1 teaspoon yogurt per toast. Drizzle each with a little
maple syrup, then load on the lemon-infused berries.
Serve immediately.

EASY TIP

Vanilla-flavoured soya yogurt is available in large
supermarkets, and it gives a sweet contrast to the
lemon-infused berries. If you don't have any available,
stir ¼ teaspoon good-quality vanilla extract into the
yogurt, or use coconut yogurt.

Chocolate houmous

MAKES 1 SMALL BOWL

1 x 400g (14oz) can of chickpeas (garbanzo beans), drained and thoroughly rinsed in hot water

1 rounded tbsp cocoa powder

4 tbsp maple syrup

2 tbsp good-quality tahini

2 tbsp soya milk

1 tsp good-quality vanilla extract

Take your love of houmous to the next level with this sweet version that everyone will love! Serve with pretzels, strawberries, bread sticks and vegan marshmallows.

1 Add all the ingredients to a high-powered jug blender or a food processor and blitz until smooth.

2 Spoon into a serving bowl.

EASY TIP
Rinsing the canned chickpeas in hot water helps to soften them, making blitzing in a blender or food processor easier.

Strawberry fairy delight

SERVES 4

60g (½ cup) icing (confectioners') sugar

liquid from 1 x 400g (14oz) can of chickpeas (garbanzo beans)

½ tsp cream of tartar

1 tsp good-quality vanilla extract

4 rounded tbsp smooth strawberry jam

Have a spoonful of the past with this vegan version of a retro British classic dessert. The whipped, moussy base is created with aquafaba, the liquid from a can of chickpeas! It works as an excellent egg substitute, and means nothing is wasted from that can of chickpeas (keep the chickpeas for another recipe).

1 Add the icing sugar and chickpea water to a stand mixer bowl, then whisk on high for 5 minutes.

2 Spoon in the cream of tartar, vanilla extract and 3 tablespoons of the strawberry jam, then whisk for a further 10 minutes until whipped and light.

3 Drizzle through the remaining strawberry jam then serve immediately.

EASY TIP

Smooth strawberry jam is available in supermarkets, or heat any strawberry jam in a pan over a low heat until it becomes liquid, then strain through a fine sieve.

Frozen pineapple whip

SERVES 4

400g (14oz) frozen pineapple

1 x 400ml (14fl oz) can of full-fat coconut milk

100ml (scant ½ cup) orange juice

2 tbsp thick coconut yogurt

Make this quick, soft-serve pineapple whip for a taste of the summer, no matter what season it actually is. For a boozy, adult-only version, drizzle in a little rum before blitzing.

1 Add the frozen pineapple, coconut milk, orange juice and coconut yogurt to a high-powered jug blender and blitz on high until it reaches a smooth, whipped texture.

2 Spoon into serving bowls, or spoon into a piping bag with a nozzle attachment and pipe into ice-cream cones.

EASY TIP
You can find frozen pineapple in supermarkets, or chop a pineapple into chunks and freeze for 12 hours before using in this recipe.

Instant raspberry sorbet

SERVES 4

250g (2 cups) frozen raspberries

2 tbsp vanilla soya yogurt

juice of 1 unwaxed lemon

Balanced, refreshing and fruity, this raspberry sorbet can be made in just a few moments. Serve alone with a few fresh mint leaves, or on the side of any hot dessert.

1 Allow the frozen raspberries to defrost slightly, for about 5–6 minutes.

2 Spoon the raspberries into a high-powered jug blender and add the soya yogurt and lemon juice. Blitz at intervals to create a smooth sorbet, then scoop into bowls. Serve immediately.

EASY TIP

Vanilla-flavoured soya yogurt is available in large supermarkets. If you don't have any available, use plain soya yogurt and a tablespoon of maple syrup for sweetness.

Mango and coconut syllabub

SERVES 4

2 large ripe mangoes, peeled, stoned and flesh roughly chopped

zest and juice of 1 unwaxed lime

1 tbsp maple syrup

8 rounded tbsp thick coconut yogurt

1 tsp desiccated (dried, shredded) coconut

This quick dessert is simple to put together for a light, summery dessert. You'll find thick coconut yogurt in supermarkets; choose varieties with a high percentage of coconut milk instead of water as a main ingredient for the creamiest texture and freshest flavour.

1 Add the mango flesh to a high-powered jug blender with the lime zest, lime juice and maple syrup. Blitz on high until smooth and thick.

2 Spoon into small serving glasses, alternating with the coconut yogurt.

3 Scatter the desiccated coconut over the top of each syllabub then serve.

EASY TIP

The mango purée can be prepared up to 2 days in advance when kept in the fridge, for a quick and easy dessert.

Apple pie quesadilla

SERVES 2

2 large green apples, coarsely grated

2 tbsp maple syrup

pinch of ground cinnamon

1 tbsp sultanas (golden raisins)

2 large white tortilla wraps

pinch of demerara sugar

What can be better than sweet, hot apple pie? This hybrid of a quesadilla and an apple pie, of course! Serve with vegan ice cream, or with vanilla custard (page 272).

1 Stir together the grated apples, maple syrup, cinnamon and sultanas in a bowl.

2 Heat a griddle (grill) pan over a medium heat.

3 Spread the apple mixture over one of the tortilla wraps and carefully place it in the hot griddle pan. Lay over the other tortilla wrap and cook for 3–4 minutes.

4 Place a large plate over the pan and invert the pan to tip the quesadilla onto it. Return the pan to the heat, then slide the quesadilla back into the pan, uncooked side down. Cook for a further 3–4 minutes.

5 Remove from the pan and slice into 4 wedges. Sprinkle with a pinch of demerara sugar and serve hot.

EASY TIP

If you struggle with turning a quesadilla in the pan, follow my advice above for fuss-free flipping!

Mexican hot chocolate

SERVES 2

500ml (2 cups) oat milk

80g (3oz) good-quality dark chocolate, broken into even pieces (ensure dairy-free)

1 tsp soft light brown sugar

1 tsp good-quality vanilla extract

1 cinnamon stick

small pinch of dried chilli flakes

pinch of grated nutmeg

There's no better way to warm up than with this gently spiced hot chocolate, made using melted dark chocolate, cinnamon, nutmeg and a hint of dried chilli.

1 Heat the oat milk, dark chocolate and sugar in a large pan over a low-medium heat, then add the vanilla extract, cinnamon stick, chilli flakes and nutmeg.

2 Simmer for 5–6 minutes, whisking constantly until gently frothy.

3 Pour into mugs and serve hot.

EASY TIP

I love the creamy taste of oat milk in this hot chocolate, but blended coconut milk, almond milk and sweetened soya milk are great alternatives.

Chocolate orange mousse

SERVES 2

340g (12oz) silken tofu

100g (3½oz) dark chocolate chips or chunks (ensure dairy-free)

4 tbsp maple syrup

1 tbsp orange liqueur (ensure vegan)

1 tsp good-quality vanilla extract

These divine little pots have a decadent flavour combination of chocolate and orange. I love the subtle boozy hint, but feel free to replace with a teaspoon of good-quality natural orange extract. Make sure that you use silken tofu, as firm tofu will not create the desired bubbly mousse texture.

1 Add the silken tofu to a high-powered jug blender and blitz on high until smooth, or use a stick blender to blitz the silken tofu in a bowl.

2 Add the dark chocolate pieces to a heatproof bowl, then melt over a pan of simmering water, ensuring the base of the bowl does not touch the water. Stir occasionally until the chocolate has melted into a shiny liquid, then carefully pour into the blended tofu.

3 Stir in the maple syrup, orange liqueur and vanilla extract, then blend again to ensure the mixture is silky smooth and fully combined.

4 Spoon into ramekin dishes or pots, then chill in the fridge for at least 4 hours or overnight until set.

EASY TIP

The mousse requires some time to set in the fridge, so it can be prepared a day in advance. Sprinkle with unwaxed orange zest just before serving, if you like.

Rocky road

MAKES ABOUT 10

120g (½ cup) vegan butter

200g (7oz) dark chocolate, broken into even pieces (ensure dairy-free)

3 tbsp golden syrup

200g (7oz) vegan digestive biscuits (graham crackers)

100g (1 cup) vegan mini marshmallows

2 tbsp glacé cherries, roughly chopped

icing (confectioners') sugar, for dusting

These fun, chocolatey squares are perfect for sharing at any special occasion, and only take 15 minutes to prepare! Just whip up a batch then pop in the fridge until needed. You'll find vegan marshmallows in some supermarket free-from aisles, health food stores and online vegan retailers. Many brands of digestive biscuits contain vegetable oil instead of butter, but always check the ingredients before you buy, or use another variety of vegan biscuit.

1 Line a small baking tin with baking parchment.

2 In a large pan, melt the vegan butter, dark chocolate and golden syrup over a low heat for 4–5 minutes until combined. Remove from the heat and allow to cool for a couple of minutes.

3 Roughly break the digestive biscuits into small, uneven pieces (the easiest way is to put into a ziplock bag and bash with a rolling pin). Stir the broken biscuits, marshmallows and cherries into the chocolate mixture until coated. Spoon the mixture into the lined baking tin, then chill in the fridge for 3–4 hours until set.

4 Dust with a little icing sugar before serving.

EASY TIP

Throw in a handful of pretzels, popcorn or dried cranberries for endless variations.

Sweet loaded nachos with marshmallows

SERVES 4

2 large white tortilla wraps, sliced into rough triangles

1 tbsp vegan butter, softened at room temperature

1 tsp granulated sugar

pinch of ground cinnamon

2 tbsp dark chocolate chips (ensure dairy-free)

2 tbsp vegan mini marshmallows

handful of blueberries

Everyone will love tucking into these cinnamon sugar tortillas, loaded with melted chocolate chips, vegan marshmallows and blueberries – and they're ready in under 15 minutes! Serve as a sharing plate, with vegan ice cream to dip.

1 Preheat the oven to 180°C/350°F/gas mark 4.

2 Arrange the tortilla triangles across one or two baking sheets, ensuring they don't overlap. Use a pastry brush to sweep over a little softened vegan butter. Sprinkle with sugar and cinnamon.

3 Bake in the oven for 5 minutes, then carefully remove. Scatter over the chocolate chips, marshmallows and blueberries, then return to the oven for a further 4–5 minutes until the sweet tortillas are light golden, and the chocolate chips have gently melted.

EASY TIP
You'll find dairy-free chocolate chips and gelatine-free marshmallows in the free-from aisle in many supermarkets, or at health food stores. Many online vegan food retailers also stock these items.

Cloudy apple and elderflower jellies

SERVES 4

500ml (2 cups) good-quality cloudy apple juice (I use Copella)

2 tsp elderflower cordial

pinch of caster (superfine) sugar

2 tsp agar agar flakes

These light and fruity jellies are perfect to enjoy on a summer's day. Choose good-quality, cloudy apple juice for the best flavour, and a dash of elderflower cordial.

1 Pour the apple juice into a pan and bring to a simmer over a low heat. Stir in the cordial, sugar and agar agar flakes and cook for 5–6 minutes until the agar agar flakes have dissolved.

2 Pour into jelly moulds, then refrigerate overnight, or for at least 6 hours, to allow the mixture to set.

3 Remove the jellies from the fridge and place the containers in a bowl of hot water for up to a minute, to make removal easier. Place the moulds on serving plates and gently shake to allow the jellies to slide onto the plates. Serve immediately.

EASY TIP

If it's elderflower season, serve these jellies with a sprig of elderflower on top, for a goregous, dinner party dessert!

Vanilla custard

SERVES 4

1 good-quality vanilla pod (bean)

500ml (2 cups) sweetened soya milk

small pinch of ground turmeric

2 tbsp caster (superfine) sugar

2 tbsp cornflour (cornstarch)

Although there are many brands of vegan custard available in supermarkets, making your own is not only easy, but extra delicious. Creamy, sweet and flecked with vanilla, this custard is perfect served hot over chai roasted rhubarb crumble (page 227).

1 Slit the vanilla pod in half lengthways and scoop out the small seeds into a large pan. Add the empty vanilla pod too and stir in the soya milk and turmeric. Simmer over a medium heat for 3–4 minutes, then remove and discard the vanilla pod.

2 Spoon in the sugar and cornflour and simmer for 20 minutes, using a balloon whisk to mix frequently, until the custard has thickened.

3 Remove from the heat and whisk vigorously. Allow to stand for 5 minutes to thicken further.

EASY TIP

A small pinch of ground turmeric gives this custard the traditional colour (in lieu of egg yolks) but it's equally wonderful without it.

Olive oil shortcrust pastry

**MAKES ENOUGH FOR
1 TART OR PIE**

250g (2 cups) plain (all-purpose) flour

6 tbsp good-quality olive oil

pinch of sea salt

I'm a huge fan of shop-bought pastry. From filo to puff, the majority of brands use vegetable oil instead of dairy, making it vegan-friendly. Sometimes, however, it's nice to make your own simple shortcrust pastry from scratch. I use olive oil instead of vegan butter for a luxuriously crumbly texture and slightly fruity flavour that works well with both sweet and savoury dishes.

1 Combine the flour and sea salt in a mixing bowl, then gradually spoon in the olive oil, using a fork to create a breadcrumb texture within the mixture.

2 Gradually pour in 50ml (3 tbsp + 1 tsp) cold water and bring together to form a pastry dough using your hands. Wrap in cling film (plastic wrap) and refrigerate for 30 minutes before rolling out.

EASY TIP
When using the pastry to make a tart, roll out the pastry using a rolling pin, then press into a pie dish. Use baking beans or dried pulses to blind bake the pastry for 20 minutes at 180°C/350°F/gas mark 4, before adding a filling of your choice and baking until set.

Sides &
Useful Bits

Jerk, coconut and lime butter corn on the cob

SERVES 4

1 tsp jerk seasoning

pinch of dried chilli flakes

2 tsp desiccated (dried, shredded) coconut

zest and juice of ½ unwaxed lime

4 rounded tbsp vegan butter

4 corn on the cob

small handful of coriander (cilantro), very finely chopped

generous pinch of sea salt

Summery, spicy and oh-so satisfying, this buttery corn on the cob is perfect for a barbecue or served with a green salad. You'll find pre-blended jerk seasoning in supermarkets; add more or fewer chilli flakes into the butter depending on the intensity of heat you prefer.

1 In a bowl, stir together the jerk seasoning, chilli flakes, coconut, lime zest and juice. Stir in the butter and mix until combined. Chill in the fridge for 20–25 minutes.

2 In the meantime, bring a large pan of water to the boil over a medium-high heat. Use tongs to place the corn on the cob in the pan and cook for 8–10 minutes until tender, then drain.

3 Rub 1 tablespoon of the spiced butter over each cooked corn on the cob and scatter with coriander and sea salt. Serve hot.

EASY TIP
The spiced butter can be frozen in advance then gently defrosted before use. Great for when you need to use up those store cupboard ingredients!

Tangy mustard and apple slaw

SERVES 4

---

3 tbsp vegan mayonnaise

1 tsp English mustard

2 carrots, peeled and grated

¼ red cabbage, very finely chopped

¼ red onion, finely diced

2 green apples, very thinly sliced

small handful of sultanas (golden raisins)

Vegan coleslaws are now readily available in most supermarkets, but what sets this special slaw apart from the rest is sweet, crisp apples and sultanas in a creamy, mustardy sauce. Delicious served with speedy chickpeas burgers (page 160) or as an addition to any simple salad.

1 Stir the vegan mayonnaise and mustard together in a large bowl.

2 Add the carrots, cabbage, red onion, apples and sultanas and stir until coated in the mustard mayonnaise.

EASY TIP
This slaw is best used within 12 hours of making, to keep the apples crisp and fresh.

Cheat's pink pickled onions

SERVES 2 GENEROUSLY

---

1 red onion, thinly sliced

150ml (generous ½ cup) apple cider vinegar

½ tsp dried chilli flakes

zest of 1 unwaxed lime

generous pinch of sea salt

Do you ever wish you had the time to make those pretty pink pickles? This is a cheat's version, ready in just 15 minutes but they'll be even more delicious if you leave them to infuse for an hour! The recipe is easy to double or triple up, too. Serve with easiest ever dhal (page 168) or as a tangy addition to a sandwich.

1 Add the sliced red onion to a bowl and cover with boiling water. Cook in the microwave for 3 minutes until softened, then drain.

2 Pour over the vinegar and stir in the chilli flakes, lime zest and sea salt. Allow to infuse for at least 10 minutes before enjoying.

EASY TIP
These pickles will keep for up to a week in a sterilized jar in the fridge.

Paprika potato rounds

SERVES 2

2 large baking potatoes, scrubbed clean

2 tbsp sunflower oil

1 tsp smoked paprika

pinch of dried thyme

small handful of flat-leaf parsley, finely chopped

generous pinch of sea salt

These smoky, crisp potatoes are unexpectedly easy to make, and delicious as a hot snack on their own, or as a tasty addition to any meal. Serve as a side dish to Spanish chickpea and olive stew (page 144), or as an alternative to rice with sweet potato, beer and lime chilli (page 211).

1 Preheat the oven to 200°C/400°F/gas mark 6 and line two baking trays with baking parchment. Cut the potatoes into slices, about 3mm (⅛in) thick.

2 In a mixing bowl, whisk together the sunflower oil, smoked paprika and thyme until combined.

3 Use a pastry brush to lightly coat the potato slices, then lay each slice on the baking trays.

4 Bake in the oven for 22–25 minutes until the edges are golden and crisp. Sprinkle with sea salt and chopped flat-leaf parsley before serving hot.

EASY TIP
Leave the skin on the potato slices for extra crispiness and a rustic appearance.

Sticky barbecue wings

SERVES 4

200ml (generous ¾ cup) barbecue sauce (ensure vegan)

2 tbsp sunflower oil

1 tsp garlic powder

1 tsp smoked paprika

½ tsp dried chilli flakes

100g (2 cups) panko breadcrumbs

1 medium cauliflower, broken into bite-sized florets with some stem remaining

These sticky barbecue cauliflower wings are so simple to create, but are packed with flavour. Use shop-bought barbecue sauce and add in extra flavours of garlic, smoked paprika and chilli. Panko breadcrumbs give an extra crisp bite, and they are available in most supermarkets. Serve with cooling sour cream (page 306).

1 Preheat the oven to 200°C/400°F/gas mark 6 and line two baking trays with baking parchment.

2 In a large bowl, mix together the barbecue sauce, oil, garlic powder, smoked paprika and chilli flakes until combined.

3 Spread out the panko breadcrumbs on a large plate. Dip the cauliflower florets into the barbecue sauce mix, shake off any excess, then roll in the panko breadcrumbs. When the florets are coated, place on the lined baking sheet. Repeat until each floret is coated.

4 Bake in the oven for 15 minutes. Carefully remove from the oven, use a spatula to turn the florets, then bake again for 10–15 minutes until the breadcrumbs are evenly golden. Serve hot.

EASY TIP

Serve straight from the oven to keep the breadcrumb coating extra crisp. The barbecue glaze can be made up to 3 days in advance.

Roasted patatas bravas

SERVES 4

---

1 x 400g (14oz) can of chopped tomatoes

2 tsp hot paprika

½ tsp dried thyme

pinch of dried chilli flakes

2 garlic cloves, very thinly sliced

pinch of sugar

700g (1½lb) new potatoes, halved

handful of flat-leaf parsley, finely chopped

generous pinch each of sea salt and black pepper

What's better than Spanish-style potatoes? Roasted, skin-on new potatoes, cooked in one tray with a paprika-infused sauce. Serve as tapas, with olives and antipasti, or as a spicy side to any midweek supper. The hardest part is ensuring they actually make it to the table (they're very moreish, and you *obviously* must test a couple before serving!).

1 Preheat the oven to 200°C/400°F/gas mark 6.

2 In a jug, mix together the tomatoes, paprika, thyme, chilli flakes, garlic and sugar. Pour the mixture into a large, deep roasting tray.

3 Place the halved new potatoes in the tray, then loosely cover with foil. Bake in the oven for 30 minutes, then remove the foil and roast for a further 30 minutes until the potatoes are golden.

4 Remove from the oven and scatter with chopped flat-leaf parsley. Season with sea salt and pepper. Serve hot or cold.

EASY TIP
These cooked potatoes will last for up to 3 days when kept in the fridge in a sealed container.

Low and slow roasted tomatoes

Mint and lemon crushed peas

SERVES 2

SERVES 4

10 large tomatoes

2 tbsp balsamic vinegar

2 tbsp sunflower oil

2 sprigs of thyme

400g (2²/₃ cups) frozen peas

1 tbsp vegan butter

zest and juice of 1 unwaxed lemon

small handful of mint leaves, very finely chopped

generous pinch of sea salt

Slow roasting tomatoes brings out a deep, intense flavour, and is a great way to use up any tomatoes left at the back of the fridge. Serve as part of mezze, hot or cold with salad, or stirred through pasta for a simple yet delicious supper.

Freshen up traditional chip shop-style mushy peas by using garden peas infused with lemon and fresh mint. Serve with golden-battered tofish (page 212) and chips.

1 Preheat the oven to 160°C/325°F/ gas mark 3.

2 Arrange the tomatoes on a large baking tray and drizzle with balsamic vinegar and sunflower oil. Lay over the sprigs of thyme, then roast in the oven for 1 hour. Allow to cool or serve hot.

1 Put the peas into a pan and pour over enough boiling water to cover them. Simmer over a low heat for 10 minutes until softened.

2 Thoroughly drain, then stir in the vegan butter, lemon zest and juice. Use a potato masher to crush the peas roughly, then allow to infuse for 10 minutes.

3 Stir through the mint leaves and sea salt, then reheat over a low heat before serving.

EASY TIP

I love roasting large tomatoes, but cherry or plum tomatoes are also delicious when roasted. Simply adjust the cooking time to 45 minutes for smaller varieties.

EASY TIP

Load into a warm wrap with sweetcorn, spring onion and chilli fritters (page 140) for a fresh and filling lunch.

Smashed butterbeans

SERVES 2

1 tbsp sunflower oil

1 garlic clove, crushed

1 x 400g (14oz) can of
butterbeans, drained and
rinsed

juice of ½ unwaxed lemon

handful of dill, finely chopped

generous pinch of sea salt

**These roughly crushed butterbeans are a great
alternative to mashed potato, particularly if you prefer a
little more texture. Flavoured with lemon and dill, these
butterbeans make a perfect high-protein side dish to
sausage, apple and bean casserole (page 146).**

1 Heat the oil and garlic in a pan over a medium heat for
2 minutes until the garlic softens and infuses the oil.

2 Stir in the butterbeans until coated in the infused oil
and cook for 2 minutes to heat through.

3 Remove from the heat and use a fork to smash most of
the butterbeans. Leave some whole for texture. Stir in the
lemon juice and dill, then season to taste with sea salt.

EASY TIP

Jarred butterbeans are softer than their canned
counterparts, meaning they will 'smash' more easily.
These tend to be more expensive, which is a consideration
if they are part of your weekly food shop.

Spiced yogurt creamed spinach

SERVES 2

1 tbsp sunflower oil

2 garlic cloves, crushed

handful of pine nuts

pinch of ground cumin

pinch of grated nutmeg

pinch of ground cinnamon

250g (9oz) spinach leaves

4 rounded tbsp thick coconut yogurt

generous pinch each of sea salt and black pepper

This lighter, spiced version of creamed spinach sits perfectly with a Sunday roast, as well as being an unexpected addition to any Indian-style feast.

1 Add the oil to a frying pan and begin to heat the garlic, pine nuts, cumin, nutmeg and cinnamon over a medium heat for 1 minute, stirring constantly, until the garlic becomes fragrant and soft.

2 Add the spinach with 2 tablespoons hot water and cook for a further 2–3 minutes until the spinach begins to wilt.

3 Stir in the yogurt and heat through for 1 minute. Season to taste with salt and pepper.

EASY TIP

For a Peshwari-style dish, stir in a tablespoon of sultanas (golden raisins) and a teaspoon of desiccated (dried, shredded) coconut with the coconut yogurt.

Garlicky greens

SERES 2

1 tbsp sunflower oil

8 florets of Tenderstem broccoli

6 asparagus spears, tough ends discarded

4 generous handfuls of shredded kale

handful of frozen peas

3 garlic cloves, thinly sliced

1 tsp vegan butter

generous pinch of sea salt

Eating your greens has never been more tasty! Switch up the kale for cavolo nero, savoy cabbage or chard according to the season, and what you have available. Enjoy as a delicious side dish.

1 Heat the oil in a wok over a high heat, then throw in the broccoli, asparagus and kale. Stir-fry for 3–4 minutes until vibrant green and beginning to soften.

2 Stir in the peas and sliced garlic, then stir-fry for a further 2 minutes.

3 Remove from the heat and stir in the vegan butter until melted. Season to taste with sea salt.

EASY TIP

For a quick and easy meal, stir these garlicky greens through pasta, or serve with tofu-fried rice (page 185).

Root gratin

SERVES 4

Suitable for freezing

4 baking potatoes, peeled and thinly sliced into rounds

4 carrots, peeled and thinly sliced

1 tbsp sunflower oil

2 garlic cloves, crushed

1 tsp dried sage

250ml (1 cup) soya single (light) cream

generous pinch each of sea salt and black pepper

I've been known to serve this side dish as a main course, with some winter leaves snipped from the garden on the side. Perfect comfort food that will brighten even the greyest of days.

1 Preheat the oven to 200°C/400°F/gas mark 6.

2 In a gratin dish or deep roasting tray, arrange a layer of potato slices followed by a layer of carrot slices. Repeat until the tray is filled. Cover the dish loosely with foil, then bake in the oven for 30 minutes.

3 Meanwhile, heat the sunflower oil in a small pan set over a low-medium heat and cook the garlic and sage until softened and fragrant. Pour in the soya cream and stir until combined with the garlic and sage. Season to taste with sea salt, then remove from the heat.

4 Carefully remove the gratin dish from the oven and discard the foil. Pour over the cream mixture, then return the dish to the oven for 30–35 minutes until the top is golden.

5 Season with plenty of black pepper.

EASY TIP

Add slices of butternut squash, pumpkin and parsnip for variations to see you through the colder months.

Zero-waste bubble and squeak

SERVES 2

3 tbsp sunflower oil

1 leek, thinly sliced

2 leaves of savoy cabbage, finely shredded

1 carrot, grated

about 4 rounded tbsp leftover mashed potatoes (prepared with non-dairy milk and vegan butter)

generous pinch each of sea salt and black pepper

Don't let that leftover mashed potato go to waste! Stir in some essential vegetables for extra flavour (feel free to use up what you have available) and cook until golden and crisp. The perfect Monday night supper, served with onion and thyme gravy (page 309) or enjoy as a simple side dish.

1 Heat 1 tablespoon of the oil in a frying pan over a high heat, then add the leek, cabbage and carrot. Cook for 2 minutes until the vegetables begin to soften, then remove from the heat.

2 Spoon the hot vegetables into a bowl with the leftover mashed potatoes and season generously with sea salt and black pepper. Stir together to combine.

3 Heat another tablespoon of oil in the same frying pan, then spoon the mashed potato mixture into the pan, use a wooden spoon to press down until flat and smooth. Cook over a high heat for 5–6 minutes until a golden crust has formed.

4 Remove from the heat and place a plate over the pan. Flip the semi-cooked bubble and squeak onto the plate, and put the pan back onto the heat with the remaining tablespoon of oil. Return the bubble and squeak to the pan and cook the uncooked side for another 5 minutes until golden.

EASY TIP

For added flavour, rub the cool, dry pan with a garlic clove before heating the oil.

INGREDIENTS 5

Fail-safe roast potatoes

SERVES 4

8 tbsp sunflower oil

4 large baking potatoes, peeled and quartered

1 tbsp plain (all-purpose) flour

generous pinch of sea salt

The perfect roast potato may seem like a tricky task to master, but it is in fact very simple. This recipe is tried and tested, on most weekends in my home. Serve hot from the oven with your Sunday lunch.

1 Preheat the oven to 200°C/400°F/gas mark 6.

2 Spoon the oil into a deep roasting tray, then place in the oven for 10 minutes to heat while you prepare the potatoes.

3 Add the potato quarters to a large pan and pour over enough boiling water to cover them completely. Parboil for 5 minutes, then thoroughly drain, returning the potatoes to the pan.

4 Spoon the flour over the potatoes, then place a lid on the pan. Shake the pan vigorously to coat all surfaces of the potatoes.

5 Carefully remove the roasting tray of hot oil from the oven. Use tongs to place each potato in the oil, turning to coat every side of the potato in oil.

6 Roast in the oven for 40 minutes, then increase the heat to 220°C/425°F/gas mark 7 for a further 10 minutes. Season with sea salt just before serving.

EASY TIP
Fluffy potatoes such as King Edward and Maris Piper make the best roast potatoes.

Cider-battered onion rings

SERVES 4

150g (1¼ cups) self-raising flour

160ml (¾ cup) chilled (hard) cider (ensure vegan)

400ml (generous 1½ cups) sunflower oil, for frying

2 large onions, thinly sliced and separated into rings

pinch of sea salt

Pub-style onion rings are always a winner, especially with this crispy, subtly boozy batter. Serve with charred mushroom steaks (page 215), or as a snack with a bowl of mustard for dipping.

1 In a large bowl, mix together the flour and salt, then whisk in the cider to form a smooth batter.

2 Meanwhile, heat the oil in a large pan over a medium heat. Test if the oil is hot enough to fry by dripping in some of the batter – if it turns golden and rises to the surface, the oil is at the optimum temperature.

3 Working in batches so you don't overcrowd the pan, dip the rings of onion into the batter to coat, then use tongs to carefully place them in the hot oil. Cook for 3–4 minutes until golden and crisp, then remove with tongs or a slotted spoon. Drain on kitchen paper. Serve hot.

EASY TIP

Not all cider is vegan as some contain ingredients such as animal-derived colourants and gelatine, so check the ingredients before you buy, or use an online resource to check vegan-friendly cider varieties.

Roasted broccoli with orange and almonds

SERVES 2

200g (7oz) Tenderstem broccoli

1 tbsp sunflower oil

pinch of dried chilli flakes

1 rounded tbsp flaked (slivered) almonds

zest of ½ unwaxed orange

generous pinch of sea salt

Roasted broccoli is a taste revelation, with a rich flavour and gently crisp florets. For me, it is the ultimate way to cook this vegetable. Team with toasted almonds and orange zest for an exciting side dish or warm salad.

1 Preheat the oven to 200°C/400°F/gas mark 6.

2 Arrange the broccoli florets on a baking tray and drizzle with sunflower oil. Sprinkle over the chilli flakes, then roast in the oven for 10 minutes.

3 Carefully remove from the oven and scatter with the flaked almonds. Return the tray to the oven for a further 5–10 minutes until the almonds are toasted.

4 Remove from the oven and sprinkle over the orange zest. Season with sea salt just before serving.

EASY TIP

Tenderstem or purple-sprouting broccoli means less waste and less preparation, but regular broccoli works well too.

Herby stuffed cabbage leaves

SERVES 4

200g (1 cup) basmati rice

generous handful of mint leaves, finely chopped

generous handful of dill, finely chopped

juice of 1 unwaxed lemon

10 dark green cabbage leaves

generous pinch of sea salt

Make these for your next dinner party, for a sharing dish that everyone will love. Prepare the rice and cabbage rolls in advance, then cook just before serving.

1 Add the basmati rice to a pan and cover with 400ml (generous 1½ cups) boiling water. Simmer for 12–15 minutes until tender. In the meantime, preheat the oven to 180°C/350°F/gas mark 4.

2 Carefully spoon the rice into a large bowl and stir through the chopped mint and dill. Stir in the lemon juice until combined with the rice and herbs. Season to taste with sea salt.

3 Lay out a cabbage leaf. Spoon 1 tablespoon of the herbed rice into the centre of the leaf, then fold the long sides inwards to meet in the centre. Then start rolling neatly from a short side until you form a sealed parcel. Place the stuffed leaf in a baking tray and repeat until you've used all of the leaves. Pack the stuffed leaves tightly next to each other in the baking tray and pour in 200ml (¾ cup) boiling water. Cover loosely with foil, then place in the oven for 30 minutes.

4 Carefully remove from the oven and allow to stand for a few minutes before serving.

EASY TIP
Throw in additional herbs such as flat-leaf parsley, or toasted pine nuts, for endless flavour variations.

Bombay new potatoes

SERVES 4

500g (1lb 2oz) new potatoes

3 tbsp sunflower oil

1 tsp mustard seeds

1 tsp fennel seeds

1 tsp ground turmeric

½ tsp mild chilli powder

½ tsp paprika

handful of cherry tomatoes

1 red chilli, deseeded and thinly sliced

handful of coriander (cilantro), roughly torn

pinch of sea salt

These spiced potatoes are everyone's favourite Indian-style side dish! They are fantastic with easiest ever dhal (page 168) but also taste wonderful served chilled with a fresh, green salad on a summer's day.

1 Bring a large pan of water to the boil over a medium-high heat, then tip in the new potatoes. Boil for 20 minutes until tender.

2 Drain and rinse with cold water until the potatoes are cool enough to cut in half. Ensure all of the water is drained away.

3 Return the pan to the heat and spoon in the sunflower oil. Sprinkle in the mustard seeds and fennel seeds and cook for 2 minutes until they start to become brown.

4 Stir in the turmeric, chilli powder, paprika and cherry tomatoes, then cook for 4–5 minutes, stirring frequently to coat the potatoes in the spice mix and avoid sticking.

5 Remove from the heat and scatter over the red chilli and coriander. Season with sea salt.

EASY TIP

The new potatoes can be cooked up to 2 days in advance then kept in the fridge until ready to use.

Mixed tempura

SERVES 4

400ml (generous 1½ cups) sunflower oil, for frying

100g (scant 1 cup) plain (all-purpose) flour

50g (½ cup) cornflour (cornstarch)

½ tsp baking powder

200ml (generous ¾ cup) ice-cold sparkling water

4 florets of Tenderstem broccoli

1 carrot, peeled and evenly sliced

8 button mushrooms

1 red (bell) pepper, deseeded and evenly sliced

It's often believed that tempura is tricky to make, but it couldn't be any more simple! The key to tempura perfection is to use ice-cold sparkling water in the batter, and by contrast, to ensure the oil for deep-frying is shimmering hot. Delicious as a starter to any eastern-style feast.

1 Begin to heat the oil in a large, heavy-based pan while you prepare the batter.

2 In a wide bowl, combine the flour, cornflour and baking powder. Stir in the sparkling water and use a balloon whisk to gently beat until smooth.

3 Check the oil is hot enough by dropping in a few drops of the batter; if it sizzles immediately it is ready. Dip the broccoli, carrot, mushrooms and pepper slices into the batter and shake off any excess. Using a slotted spoon, add a few of the vegetables to the very hot oil. Do not add too many at a time, as they will mass together. Deep-fry for 2–3 minutes until the batter has become crisp and puffed.

4 Carefully remove from the hot oil and drain on kitchen paper while you cook the remaining vegetables. Serve hot with your choice of dipping sauce.

EASY TIP
Mix light soy sauce and dried chilli flakes for a simple and delicious dipping sauce.

Sticky noodles

SERVES 2

---

1 tbsp sunflower oil

8 sugarsnap peas, sliced lengthways

handful of frozen or fresh edamame beans

300g (10oz) soft ready-to-wok noodles (ensure egg-free)

2 rounded tbsp orange marmalade

2 spring onions (scallions), finely chopped

generous pinch of sea salt

Sticky, sweet, zesty and slippery, these noodles are perfect served with any Chinese-inspired main course. Or simply enjoy as a satisfying, addictive snack.

1 Heat the oil in a wok over a medium high heat, then throw in the sugarsnap peas and edamame beans. Stir-fry for 2–3 minutes until softened.

2 Add the noodles and marmalade, then stir-fry for a further 2 minutes until sticky.

3 Remove from the heat and scatter with spring onions. Season to taste with sea salt.

EASY TIP

Ready-to-wok noodles can be a little difficult to separate, meaning some of the noodles will become broken in the wok. Simply soak the noodles in a bowl of boiling water for a couple of minutes before draining and adding to the wok.

Easy pilau rice

SERVES 4

350g (1¾ cups) white basmati rice

¼ tsp ground turmeric

1 cinnamon stick

2 bay leaves

2 cardamom pods

generous pinch of sea salt

This is the recipe for pilau rice that I use at home, because it's fail-safe, easy and fragrant. Serve with any Indian-style curry – it's particularly delicious with cauliflower korma with sultanas (page 171).

1 Add the rice, turmeric, cinnamon stick, bay leaves and cardamom pods to a large pan then pour over 500ml (2 cups) boiling water. Simmer, uncovered, over a medium heat for 10 minutes, stirring occasionally until most of the water has been absorbed.

2 Remove from the heat, then securely place a lid on the pan. Leave to stand for 10 minutes.

3 Remove the pan lid and use a fork to separate the rice strands. Season to taste with sea salt.

EASY TIP

I love to serve this pilau rice in a large serving bowl for everyone to help themselves. It looks beautiful served with the whole spices in, but do remind guests not to eat them!

Crispy Chinese kale

SERVES 2

180g (6oz) shredded kale, tough stems discarded

2 tbsp sunflower oil

1 tsp light soy sauce

1 tsp granulated sugar

generous pinch of Chinese five-spice

2 tsp sesame seeds

Master the art of crispy baked kale and you'll never look back! Serve as a stand-alone snack, or as part of a Chinese-inspired feast.

1 Preheat the oven to 180°C/350°F/gas mark 4.

2 In a large bowl, mix together the kale, oil and soy sauce, then scatter through the sugar, Chinese five-spice and sesame seeds. Stir through to evenly distribute.

3 Lay the kale out evenly across two baking trays. Bake in the oven for 9–10 minutes until crisp.

EASY TIP
Use a bag of pre-chopped kale for this recipe to save you time chopping large leaves.

Pitta crackers

SERVES 4

2 white pitta breads, sliced into small triangles

1 tbsp sunflower oil

pinch of fennel seeds

pinch of dried mixed herbs

pinch of sea salt

Use up those last pitta breads in the pack to make these perfect crackers. Allow the crackers to cool for at least 20 minutes, as they become crisper the cooler they get.

1 Preheat the oven to 180°C/350°F/gas mark 4.

2 Arrange the pitta triangles across two baking trays then drizzle with sunflower oil. Rub in to cover each triangle. Sprinkle over the fennel seeds and dried mixed herbs, then bake in the oven for 8–10 minutes until lightly golden.

3 Remove from the oven and allow to stand for at least 20 minutes to become crispy as they cool. Season with sea salt.

EASY TIP
Wholemeal pitta breads give a nuttier flavour, but will need a couple of minutes more to cook in the oven.

Pea and avocado guacamole

SERSES 4

1 avocado, peeled and stoned

150g (1 cup) frozen or fresh peas (defrosted if using frozen)

1 small red onion, very finely diced

1 ripe tomato, deseeded and finely chopped

small handful of flat-leaf parsley, finely chopped

juice of 1 unwaxed lime

generous pinch of sea salt

Reduce the cost of homemade guacamole with this fresh and thrifty recipe. Peas add extra flavour and protein, as well as a new flavour level. I love a chunky guacamole, but if you prefer a smoother texture, simply blitz the peas and avocado in a blender for a few seconds.

1 Put the avocado and peas into a large bowl and use a potato masher to crush until semi-smooth.

2 Stir in the red onion, tomato and parsley, then squeeze over the lime juice. Stir until combined. Season to taste with sea salt.

EASY TIP

Smooth onto slices of thick sourdough toast, or serve with beer and lime chilli (page 211).

Fresh tomato salsa

SERVES 4

300g (2 cups) cherry tomatoes, diced

1 small red onion, finely diced

handful of flat-leaf parsley, finely chopped

handful of coriander (cilantro) leaves, finely chopped

juice of ½ unwaxed lime

generous pinch of sea salt

No weekend is complete without tortilla chips and a bowl of tomato salsa; once you try this fresh version, no shop-bought salsa will do!

1 In a bowl, stir together the diced tomatoes, red onion, parsley and coriander until evenly distributed.

2 Squeeze in the lime juice, then season with a generous pinch of sea salt.

EASY TIP
Increase the heat by topping with a few thin slices of green chilli, if you are brave enough...

Sour cream

Versatile chermoula

SERVES 4

4 rounded tbsp unsweetened soya yogurt

2 rounded tbsp plain vegan cream cheese

juice of ½ unwaxed lemon

handful of fresh chives, finely chopped

generous pinch of sea salt

Tangy, cool, creamy and thick – can sour cream get any better? In fact it can, when it's vegan-friendly and ready in under 15 minutes! Add a spoonful over sweet potato, beer and lime chilli (page 211) or as a simple filling for jacket potatoes.

1 Add the yogurt and cream cheese to a mixing bowl, then use a balloon whisk to combine fully until thickened and smooth.

2 Stir in the lemon juice and chives, then season to taste with sea salt.

EASY TIP

Choose plain unsweetened soya yogurt and plain vegan cream cheese to get the most authentic flavour from this sour cream.

MAKES 1 SMALL JAR
(ENOUGH FOR 1 LARGE TAGINE)

1 red onion, roughly quartered

2 garlic cloves

1 rounded tsp ground turmeric

1 rounded tsp ground cumin

½ tsp mild chilli powder

½ tsp smoked paprika

pinch of dried chilli flakes

pinch of ground ginger

generous handful of flat-leaf parsley

2 tbsp maple syrup

drizzle of sunflower oil

juice of 1 unwaxed lemon

generous pinch of sea salt

Use as a base for any tagine, tip over a whole cauliflower to roast, or brush over aubergine (eggplant) slices before baking.

1 Add all of the ingredients to a high-powered jug blender or food processor, then pour in 100ml (scant ½ cup) cold water. Blitz until smooth.

2 Store in the fridge in a sealed container for up to 3 days.

EASY TIP

Freeze in a tub, or in an ice-cube tray to defrost for smaller dishes such as brushing over aubergines.

Cheat's aioli

SERVES 6

4 rounded tbsp vegan mayonnaise

1 tsp Dijon mustard

2 garlic cloves, crushed

juice of ¼ unwaxed lemon

generous pinch of sea salt

Who doesn't love a rich and creamy garlic aioli? This version is all about the flavour, with none of the fuss. Spoon into wraps, serve with carrot and coriander fritters (page 83), or simply serve with crudités.

1 In a bowl, whisk together the vegan mayonnaise and Dijon mustard until combined.

2 Stir in the garlic and lemon juice, then season to taste with sea salt. Allow to infuse for at least 1 hour.

EASY TIP
Store in a clean, sealed jar in the fridge for up to a week.

Tartare sauce

SERVES 6

4 rounded tbsp vegan mayonnaise

2 small pickled gherkins, drained of vinegar and finely chopped

2 tbsp capers, drained of brine and finely chopped

handful of dill, finely chopped

juice of ¼ unwaxed lemon

Golden-battered tofish (page 212) just isn't the same without tartare sauce! This versatile sauce is also delicious served over grilled courgettes (zucchini), and perfect with antipasti paella (page 210). Keep in the fridge for up to 4 days.

1 In a bowl, stir together the mayonnaise, gherkins, capers and dill.

2 Whisk in the lemon juice until combined.

EASY TIP
Vegan mayonnaise is readily available in most supermarkets, from a range of well-known and independent brands.

Burger sauce

SERVES 4

2 rounded tbsp vegan mayonnaise

1 rounded tbsp tomato ketchup

2 small pickled gherkins, finely diced

pinch of sea salt

No vegan burger is complete without a spoonful of tangy burger sauce. This recipe is easy to double up for serving families and friends, making it the perfect condiment for any barbecue. Serve with speedy chickpea burgers (page 160).

1 Mix together the vegan mayonnaise and ketchup until combined, then stir through the diced gherkins.

2 Season to taste with sea salt.

EASY TIP
This sauce will keep for up to 5 days in the fridge in a sealed container.

Best ever pizza sauce

MAKES ENOUGH TO
COVER 2 MEDIUM PIZZAS

1 tbsp sunflower oil

2 garlic cloves, crushed

1 x 400g (14oz) can of good-quality chopped tomatoes

2 rounded tbsp tomato purée (paste)

1 tsp soft light brown sugar

2 tsp dried oregano

generous handful of basil leaves, finely chopped

generous pinch each of sea salt and black pepper

Do you ever crave that authentic pizza flavour, but can't seem to get the flavours right on your homemade pizza? Look no further than this 30-minute sauce.

1 Add the oil and garlic to a large pan, then cook over a medium heat for 2 minutes until softened and fragrant.

2 Pour in the chopped tomatoes, tomato purée, brown sugar and oregano, then cook over a medium-high heat for 25 minutes, stirring frequently until glossy.

3 Season, then remove from the heat and stir through the basil.

EASY TIP
Suitable for freezing, this will also keep in the fridge for up to 4 days.

POT · POT · POT · POT ·
1

INGREDIENTS · INGREDIENTS
5

Tomato and chilli pasta sauce

Onion and thyme gravy

SERVES 4

SERVES 4

1 tbsp sunflower oil

2 garlic cloves, crushed

½ tsp dried chilli flakes

500g (2 cups/17oz) good-quality passata (sieved tomatoes)

pinch of granulated sugar

small handful of flat-leaf parsley, chopped

generous pinch each of sea salt and black pepper

1 tbsp sunflower oil

2 onions, thinly sliced

generous pinch of brown sugar

1 tbsp plain (all-purpose) flour

400ml (generous 1½ cups) good-quality vegetable stock

1 sprig of fresh thyme

generous pinch of black pepper

This simple, freezer-friendly recipe means that you'll never have to buy a jar of pasta sauce again.

1 Heat the oil, garlic and chilli flakes in a pan over a medium heat for 2–3 minutes until the garlic has softened and the oil is infused.

2 Pour in the passata and sugar, then place a lid loosely over the pan. Cook for 10 minutes, stirring occasionally.

3 Remove from the heat and season to taste with sea salt and plenty of black pepper. Stir through the flat-leaf parsley.

Nothing beats a thick onion gravy poured over vegan sausages and perfect mashed potatoes.

1 Heat the oil in a large pan over a low-medium heat, then add the onions and cook for 10 minutes, stirring occasionally. Sprinkle in the brown sugar and cook for a further 3 minutes until the onions caramelize.

2 Stir in the flour and cook for 1 minute. Gradually stir in the stock then add the thyme sprig. Cook, stirring, for 10 minutes until thickened, then season to taste.

EASY TIP

If freezing, simply defrost, reheat and stir through any egg-free pasta of your choice, for a delicious midweek pasta arrabbiata.

EASY TIP

Pour the stock in gradually, stirring or whisking frequently to help thicken the gravy without leaving any lumps.

Five-spice cranberry sauce

SERVES 4

Suitable for freezing

zest and juice of 1 unwaxed orange

250g (2½ cups) fresh or frozen cranberries

3 tbsp caster (superfine) sugar

½ tsp Chinese five-spice

Give classic cranberry sauce an eastern twist with the addition of Chinese five-spice and orange zest. Don't just save cranberry sauce for Christmas; spoon it over roasted vegetables or enjoy in a vegan cheese sandwich.

1 Add the orange zest and juice to a pan, along with the cranberries and sugar. Cook over a medium heat for 5 minutes, stirring frequently to help break down the cranberries.

2 Stir in the Chinese five-spice and cook for 1 further minute, then remove from the heat. The sauce will thicken as it cools.

EASY TIP

Chinese five-spice is a pre-blended mix of ground cinnamon, star anise, cloves, pepper and ginger. Keep a jar in the store cupboard to sprinkle over crispy kale, or in tofu-fried rice (page 185).

Index

Acknowledgements

What a pleasure it has been to write *Easy Vegan Bible*, my sixth (and biggest) book so far. I feel like I had the easy job, however, as the book would not have come together without the team of talented and dedicated people who turned it from words in a document, into this beautiful book.

Firstly, thank you to the editorial team at Quadrille. Thank you to publishing director Sarah Lavelle for believing in me, the concept, and for all of the opportunities. Heartfelt thanks to editor Harriet Webster for your dedication, attention to detail, and for always having a smile. It is a privilege to work with you! Special thanks to copy editor Clare Sayer for another round of prompt editorial support. I'm looking forward to working with you all again.

Massive thanks to designer Emily Lapworth for the art direction and design. I loved your vision for the book throughout this process, and the results are modern, fresh and beautiful.

Thank you so much to photographer Luke Albert, food stylist Libby Silberman and assistants Grace Paul and Sophie Garwood, and prop stylist Louie Waller for the socially-distanced shoot at Studio Boardroom, during the COVID-19 pandemic. I missed working with you all in person, but really appreciated the Zoom call updates. The images are absolutely gorgeous, thank you.

I am so grateful for the hard work of senior publicist Rebecca Smedley. I always love working with you! Thank you to marketing executive Laura Eldridge for your ongoing guidance and expertise. Thank you both for championing all of the books!

Huge, ongoing thanks to my wonderful literary agent Victoria Hobbs and the team at A.M. Heath. I couldn't do this without your expert advice and guidance. I can't wait to see where the adventure takes us next.

Thank you, as always, to my amazing friends Mary-Anne, Charlotte, Louise, Amelia, Emma, Amy, Katie, Neil and Robert. I always appreciate your support, texts, calls, coffees (even remotely), and encouragement to continue when I feel under pressure. I can't wait to see you all soon. Thank you to Michael for being an honorary taste tester, and for your support, care and much appreciated trips to the coast.

To my wonderful family: Mum, Dad, Carolyne and Mark. Thank you for your abundant support, and all the practical help, decorating and renovating my new house whilst I was writing this book. What would I do without you? Thank you to Auntie May for your love and encouragement. To my beautiful twin nieces Tamzin and Tara, I hope you enjoy making these new recipes. I love you very much.

Thank you, as always, to Dudley the house rabbit, who continues to be the best writing partner any author could ever ask for.

Publishing Director
Sarah Lavelle

Editor
Harriet Webster

Copy Editor
Clare Sayer

Art Direction and Design
Emily Lapworth

Photographer
Luke Albert

Food Stylist
Libby Silberman

Prop Stylist
Louie Waller

Make-up Artist
Dani Hooker

Head of Production
Stephen Lang

Production Controller
Nikolaus Ginelli

First published in 2020 by Quadrille,
an imprint of Hardie Grant Publishing

Quadrille
52–54 Southwark Street
London SE1 1UN
quadrille.com

Text © Katy Beskow 2020
Photography © Luke Albert 2020
Design and layout © Quadrille 2020

Cataloguing in Publication Data: a catalogue record
for this book is available from the British Library.

ISBN: 978 1 78713 566 6

Printed in China